THE PHENOMENOLOGY OF SEX, LOVE, AND INTIMACY

The Phenomenology of Sex, Love, and Intimacy presents a phenomenological exploration of love as it manifests itself through sexual desires and
intimate relationships. Setting up a unique dialogue between psychology
and philosophy, Susi Ferrarello offers a perspective through which clinicians can inform their practice on diverse issues of human sexuality.

Drawing on Husserl's phenomenology, Ferrarello's analysis of love
spans a range of disciplines including psychology, theology, biology,
epistemology, and axiology, as well as areas related to gender, consent,
and political control. Combining Husserlian perspectives on ethics with
a focus on lived-experience, this text will deepen therapists' understanding of love as the subject of interdisciplinary inquiry and enable
them to locate questions of sexuality and intimacy within an academic
framework.

With key theoretical principles included to allow clinicians to think
through and clarify their practice, this book will be a valuable tool for
sex therapists, marriage and family therapists, and counselors, as well as
psychology and philosophy students alike.

Susi Ferrarello is a professor at California State University and Say-
brook University, teaching philosophy to graduate students of psychology. She holds a PhD in Philosophy from Sorbonne and an MA in
Human Rights and Political Science from the University of Bologna.

THE PHENOMENOLOGY OF SEX, LOVE, AND INTIMACY

Susi Ferrarello

Routledge
Taylor & Francis Group

NEW YORK AND LONDON

First published 2019
by Routledge
52 Vanderbilt Avenue, New York, NY 10017

and by Routledge
2 Park Square, Milton Park, Abingdon, Oxon, OX14 4RN

Routledge is an imprint of the Taylor & Francis Group, an informa business

© 2019 Taylor & Francis

Library of Congress Cataloging-in-Publication Data
A catalog record for this title has been requested

ISBN: 978-0-8153-5809-1 (hbk)
ISBN: 978-0-8153-5810-7 (pbk)
ISBN: 978-1-351-12326-6 (ebk)

Typeset in Bembo
by Wearset Ltd, Boldon, Tyne and Wear

To Fabiola Ferrarello, with love and gratitude

CONTENTS

INTRODUCTION

Sorting Out Problems

What Do We Talk About When We Talk About Love?

I never thought that love would have been the subject of my philosophical studies, partly because I always assumed that that kind of investigation would pertain to different areas of human studies, such as poetry, music, art, and the like; partly because I believed that something whose nature is so ephemeral should never be questioned, otherwise its essence would fade away. Yet, as it often happens, we cannot decide what direction our studies are going to take. A few years ago, I was invited to hold a series of lectures for a newborn program on Human Sexuality, in San Francisco. I accepted the invitation with great enthusiasm, which soon turned into a state of anxiety when I realized the breadth of study that this area would have required.

Love seems to be the main constituent of the human soul; one discipline is not enough to shed light on its essence. "Amore ipsa notitia est" Gregory the Great wrote in his Homelia in Evangelium, 2—"love itself is knowledge." The graduate and undergraduate programs on human sexuality that are burgeoning today seem to have the difficult task of educating people on a vital subject (that for reasons I cannot address here was neglected for centuries) that encompasses different disciplines and therefore requires overcoming the obsolete boundary between Geistes- and Natur-Wissenschaften. Hence, when I started preparing for these lectures I easily understood that philosophy alone was not adequate; biology, chemistry, neurology, anthropology, geography, history religion, psychology, and many more disciplines needed to be included in this conversation on love. I started collecting a vast bibliography that later on I organized by themes and concepts.

The more I read, the more I felt a strong sense of responsibility growing in me. In fact, I realized how much violence, injustice, and inequality had hidden over the centuries behind the word love. The fact that love was never duly investigated by a rigorous research paved the way for the most painful episodes in our personal and collective history. For this reason, I am grateful for all academic and non-academic programs that are currently investing energy and funds in designing curricula to train people in being responsible for the love they receive and give. Thus, this sense of gratitude led me to the decision to start writing my lectures and to organize them in a book with the hope that the material and the thoughts I collected could be of use.

After the reading phase of my work, I felt of course overwhelmed and very hesitant about the direction to take, the language to use, the discipline to privilege. It was at that point that Husserl's phenomenology came at hand. Even though I briefly referred to other phenomenologists, I preferred using his way of applying phenomenology because it was in line with the goal of my "meaning-making" analysis. According to Husserl, phenomenology is a Wissenschaftslehre: a science that organizes the knowledge collected by all the other sciences. So, in these lectures I used phenomenology as descriptive language to organize and describe what other disciplines observed about the nature of love and I used lived-experience as the point of departure for my observation and study. As the analysis unfolded I realized that what I discovered in my previous books, in particular concerning the notion of practical intentionality, could be of use here to capture and express my understanding of love. For this reason some of the parts of this book will refer to and make use of my previous work (Ferrarello, 2015, 2018).

The Names of Love

Another problem I had to face was—what kind of love did I want to talk about in these lectures? Love can take so many names that it is very easy to get lost and miss the opportunity for an actual dialogue on the topic. Love can reveal itself through affection, empathy, emotions, drives, sentiments, understanding, time, and so forth. I believe we cannot separate the essence of love from these constituents; yet I needed to identify the main signifiers in order to open up a dialogue that was understandable and acceptable to everybody.

For this reason my resolution for this book was to use the Greek language to name three main layers of love: *eros*, *philia*, and *agape*. In the
first part, I describe how desires, drives, and instincts—what Greek calls
eros—add meaning to our identity, even when they are considered
wrong and rejected by the society. Then in the second part I observe
how intimacy, in Greek *philia*, is that first necessary bond we need to
establish with ourselves and others in order to find ourselves within the
ongoing flow of meanings that fill our life. Finally, in the third part I
describe how lives come to tie themselves together with others in a
strong bond called *agape*. This bond generates a very complex layer
which can produce loss of meaning for the individual, but at the same
time generate new meanings for society. Hence, in this section it was
important for me to analyze the range of responsibilities that individuals
and society have to take in relation to this form of love. The general
organization of each section is such that it dedicates at least two chapters
to the analysis of each concept, a general theoretical one and a more
practical one in which I apply the phenomenological reading to a specific case, for example: jealousy, perversions, gender identity, and so
forth.

Intentions of the Book

This book does not seek to arrive at a final definition about the nature
of love because I do not believe in final answers. Seeking a final answer
would be against a rigorous phenomenological attitude and against my
beliefs in the infinite progress of living beings. I started writing this book
because while I was teaching I realized that we need to reflect on the
nature of love if we want human beings to grow more responsible
toward love. I thought it would be useful for the scholarly community
and for those who want to use the phenomenological method in health
and social sciences to have a path that shows them the layers that bring
together meanings and feelings in one's loving life. For this reason, in
this book I am going to discuss love as it belongs to an interconnection
of systems and I will provide a phenomenological description of love as
it manifests itself through inter-corporeal bonds, sexual desires, and
intimate relationships, that is in its material and spiritual layers. The
Greek words for love, *eros*, *philia*, and *agape*, (i.e., erotic passion, intimate
and friendly love, and universal love) will be used in order to distinguish
the different areas of manifestation of the love experience. In particular,
I will use Husserl's phenomenology and his ethics to sort out the layers
that comprise the experience of love in order to understand how

instincts and drives develop into desires, relational bonds, to finally become political subjects. The overall goal of the book is to help the reader to reflect on love as an academic subject matter in its declensions of sex, intimacy, and social love.

Structure of the Book

As written above the book is organized in three main sections, *eros*, *philia*, and *agape*. Each section includes two or three chapters. The section dedicated to *eros* examines the meaning that the erotic life has for the individual in three chapters. In the first one I focus on the intentional forces that drive the erotic life, in the second I discuss what we mean by sexual life, and in the third one, its "perversions." In the second section I discuss the primal bond that we establish with ourselves and others in three chapters; the first one is focused on the description of the bond and the remaining two chapters discuss the unifying and distancing pull of this bond through a study of intimacy and jealousy. Finally, in the third section I discuss a social form of love in two chapters, one dedicated to the study of this form of bond in a "normal" society and the other one specifically dedicated to the categories of sexual normality that are used in the society.

The first chapter examines the characteristics of intentional acts (i.e., objectivating and reflective aiming at) and how these characteristics apply to the practical component of intentional acts with the goal of displaying the theoretical foundations of the research I will conduct in the next chapters. While in Husserl's *Logical Investigations* non-intentional matter seems to be neatly distinguished from intentional matter, in *Ideas* and in the *Analyses* non-intentional matter seems to constitute a bridge for matter to become intentional and constitutive of meaning. In the *Analyses* feeling intentionality is not only that which triggers an intention; it is also an objectivating force. Hence feeling (affective) intentionality, which will be central in the analysis of love, intimate, and sexual life that I will conduct in the following chapters, seems to be an invisible layer of the intentional structure that should not remain invisible to the eyes of the phenomenologist who wants to investigate the life of the heart; this layer, in fact, represents a primordial form of objectivation that originates from affect-consciousness (*Gemütbewusstsein*, Hua XXXI, 5) and fulfills itself in the constitution of the ego. This form of objectivation awakens an ego that, as a subject of acts, can reflect upon its content-matter and distinguish itself from them in a way that constitutes itself as a meaningful whole. The primordiality of matter is not intentional in itself when it acts as the trigger for further objectivation; however, matter is intentional in the validating and affective process through which it awakens the ego and leads it to objectivate itself and its contents. Within this primordiality there is a thin intentional layer that calls for practical reflection and the constitution of meaning; this layer is what I have called—with Husserl's permission—*practical intention*; that is, the intentionality of consciousness in the mode of wakefulness (Hua XLII, 51). This practical intention is the dynamic bodily and spiritual tension that connects the three levels of love I examine in the book.

The second chapter describes how sexual life arises as an egoless hyletic (material and pre-reflective) life that is put in motion by passive intentionality, coitus intentionality, and is transformed into active intentionality, namely a meaning-giving activity. This analysis confirms how while sex represents a basic need of our intersubjective and generative life, it is enjoyable even when disconnected from this basic need because it keeps the individual in contact with the lowest organic matter of its life.

According to Husserl, on its lower level sexual life is moved by instincts, drives, impulses, and aims at the fulfillment of desiderative life that ultimately seems to be directed at the procreation. On its higher level, sexual life is moved by the not-operating and operating will which allows the transition from an hyletic egoless flow to the awakening of the ego as intersecting with other flows. On this level the ultimate goal of the sexual life is the constitution of a Mitwelt—which we might call family, state, relationship—in which the ego wakes up and builds its own life. Both levels contribute in different ways to the constitution of the sexual personality; the cycle of active acceptance or negation of some of the ongoing flow of lower instincts, drives, and impulses is what guides the formation of a habitual character. Sensuous pleasure can arise on both layers, either as fulfillment of the immediate goal of the instincts or as a fulfillment of the habitual tendency to recognize the same.

In the third chapter I discuss a case of paraphilia, using Husserl's theory of practical intentionality. I prepared the analysis using Sartre's and Nagel's phenomenological point of view: as will be seen, they condemn this lived-experience as a perversion of the natural need for mutual recognition. By means of other philosophical points of view, such as Plato's, Weil's, and Cowan's, I show how a masochistic and sadistic quality is intrinsic to the nature of love; being able to explore this quality can foster the meaning that we can gather about our lives. Hence, love, meant also as masochism and sadism can be a necessary force that pushes us toward a deeper understanding of ourselves. If we try to tame it, we would miss the opportunity to know who we really are.

The fourth chapter discusses the lower and higher layers of the spirit in order to explain how the volitional body—the moral organ of our actions—validates the feelings that lead us to intimate love. In the chapter I show how this body cannot be considered as belonging exclusively to material or immaterial layers; accordingly, every decision it makes participates in lower and higher motives. It is through these lenses that the brutal force of love and the space of intimacy that it opens up is interpreted as a vertical feeling connecting lower and higher, material and immaterial layers of us; on a lower level love is a whole of drives, instincts, desires of which cannot have a firm hold because we do not own them. In fact on this level, the subject is not even an ego yet, but is an ongoing chain of syntheses of passive matter. On the higher level, love is a meaning- and value-giving activity; it interprets the passive matter that is provided to it through the awakening of the I and validates it according to specific meanings and values that shed light on what that person actually is. The light shed on these layers forms a space of intimacy through which the person can come in contact with parts of itself that are thus far unexplored and as yet unrevealed. The brutal bonding force of love represents a unique opportunity for us to become closer to our factual existence. This involves that on the one hand, intimacy will disclose a dark place where the sensuous egoless generative web of syntheses builds a concreteness that might eventually take shape into meanings and values constitutive for the identity and sense of reality within which a person feels themself living; on the other hand, intimacy represents a retrospective reconstruction of the layers of the known intimate life as it appears to be sedimented in the habitual layers of an I. The former kind of intimacy lays the foundation for a valid, but yet dark, space in which the I can come into existence, the latter recognizes the interconnection between the layers that belong to that validity as a founding core around which life, the habitual one, constitutes itself as a meaningful vital flow.

In Chapter 5 I show how sexuality defines our existence when it involves an active choice. This choice, though, being involved in a recursive teleological structure, cannot always be conscious because our factual being is usually a mystery to us; a truth whose essence speaks to us from a transcendental space. Metaphorically speaking, I name this voice "intimacy." From the depth of our passive life the meanings that define us and constitute the condition of possibility for our existence come from intimacy, whose structure can be broken down in two main layers: a spontaneous and a transcendental one. In our lives we are constantly called on to choose whether we want to pay attention to the constitution of meanings that are going to shape the social category through which we will be recognized. In particular when we encounter cases of forced intimacy, this has a negative impact on our psychological balance. If this transcendental voice remains on the layer of passivity, it is likely that our sexual existence will be foreign and meaningless to us; if we manage to attend to this voice on an active and transcendental layer and participate in the constitution of meaning, our sexual identity will be an existential one: the fruit of a choice. Our sexual identity needs to be plastic in the sense that its telos cannot be placed in one category once and for all. To fit in an existential sexuality that is meaningful for us, we need to be free from moral and social constraints and be available to entertain an honest dialogue with our facticity.

In Chapter 6 I address the questions: What is jealousy? Is it really a feeling or is it an instinct? Does jealousy have anything to do with intimacy? Does it involve love? Does jealousy require the presence of another person?

We can say that jealousy is rooted in egoless syntheses that locate themselves on a pre-personal level; this means that jealousy is not properly about love or about an intimate relationship with another person because it arises first at a pre-personal level and it has to do with the space of intimacy that the emerging ego decides to establish with its volitional body. This means that jealousy does not necessarily involve the presence of another person, because it starts as an instinct (like many other instincts, this is the reason why Thooney found it difficult to distinguish jealousy from other states, like fear or anxiety) and its most convincing meaning remains always tied to the instinct itself. This instinct is pre-personal and pre-egoic because it is fully attached to our organic matter and calls upon that primordial life in which we are not yet fully ourselves, but we move toward in a specific direction. This direction can be understood as a hint which, if followed, can clarify the meaning of the instinct. In this state the emerging ego may interpret this instinct as jealousy, but like any interpretation of organic matter, its meaning can be further refined depending on the level of intimacy and closeness that that person entertains with his or her own body.

Chapter 7 is focused on the study of the intersubjective community as it is constituted on a pre-predicative and predicative level. I explain how love is a bonding force on a pre-predicative (lawful) level and an absolute ought on a predicative (normative) one and how the two knit together the scattered matter of being. This process of constitution around an organic and spiritual ought is brought together by the affection of time and empathy. These two kinds of affective forces reveal on both levels how the intersubjective whole is constituted as an egoless flow of synthetic matter and a reflecting egoic act of responsibility. The notion of normality flows from the interplay of these two layers as an egoless validation of the scattered matter of being and the responsible act of owning and giving meaning to that which has been validated. As it concerns the questions raised in the chapter: how does the individual's "best" become a common "best" within a normed society? How can I be at the same time a part within the community as a whole, and a whole myself? The answer lies in our deep understanding of the process of passive constitution of life and our ability and will to assign a meaning to it. From there the other questions—How can my sexuality be completely fulfilled within a normal society? How can I express my love for someone within the social web of normativity? How can a subject live an authentic life without being excessively influenced by others?—can be addressed. In fact, we build normality every day in what we passively bring within our society and in the way we decide to answer in the call of love according to our predicative mode. The choice of altering the inter-subjective community in which we live begins on a pre-predicative passive level, but it is on the predicative level that conscious meanings are constituted in the contribution of the collective notion of normality. In that sense, the agapic force of love seems to be the glue that unites the scattered matter of our being around a core of sense that each one of us continuously contributes to build according to aware (predicative) and unaware (pre-predicative) choices.

In Chapter 8 I analyze the meaning of normality and abnormality in relation to the notion of intercorporeality. I applied what emerged from my previous analysis on the case of gender identity disorder in order to show how a disembodied meaning of intersubjectivity leads to a definition of normality that obliges the individual to choose between identity or care. For this reason, as a concluding note in the chapter, I propose to use the notion of intercorporeality as complementary to construe an embodied idea of normality.

Conclusion

Through the eight chapters of the book I describe how the power of love in its positive and negative effects can impact our lives as individuals and as part of the society. Love more than anything else requires care, responsibility, phronesis (practical intention). The challenge is that its requirements are also its main constituents. So, if we do not pay attention to the requirements we risk polluting our personal and intersubjective sense of love and impoverishing the quality of our reality. For this reason, perhaps, the concluding line of Dante's Commedia points to love as a constituting structure of the whole universe: "L'amore che move il sole e l'altre stelle" (Paradiso XXXIII, 145).

1

PRACTICAL INTENTIONALITY AND *GEFÜHLSINTENTIONALITÄT*

Introduction

In this chapter I will focus on practical intentionality—a term that I believe can positively contribute to the phenomenological analysis of sex, love, and intimacy. I believe that a phenomenological exploration *Gemüt*[1] (heart),[2] in particular an Husserlian one, is as important as the analysis of *doxische Vernunft* (epistemological reason),[3] and that the exploration of practical intentionality contributes not only to a balanced view of the relationship between the two, but also to an exploration of feelings and emotions.

Husserl used the expression "practical intention"[4] (Hua VII, 34) to describe *Seinsmeinung*, i.e the intention of the being in a knowing act.[5] Scholars such as Nam-In Lee (2000) and Crowell (2013) have described practical intentionality as an ability to determine matter through Being. Nam-In Lee defined practical intentionality as a form of intentionality that determines every other form of intentionality (2000, 50). In contrast, Crowell defined practical intentionality as "a certain ability-to-be—namely, to be rational, to take responsibility for normative assessment" (2013, 275). An example of practical intention is a New Year's Eve resolution that you make without necessarily sharing its meaning with anyone else or phrasing it in a sentence.

In particular, in this chapter *I will discuss practical intentionality as a form of practical reflection and 'aiming at' that is not naïve, and hence does not equate to action* (Hua XIX, 358). Like a New Year's Eve resolution, you do not just decide to act naïvely in one direction or another, but you carefully choose what you are going to do because that is the direction that you propose to take for yourself in the New Year.

I believe that for Husserl, practical intentionality provides the ground for phenomenological ethics (Ferrarello, 2015), as well as the foundation for a meaningful analysis of intimate life. Broadly speaking I believe that practical intentionality can be usefully regarded as closely related to *phronesis* in that practical intentionality is a form of reflection that comes to expression through wakeful, aware feelings. I will expand upon this definition in the following discussion.

Moreover, I think that psychological analysis can benefit from greater focus upon practical intentionality for three reasons. First, this term gives a name to an important component of the structure of intentionality which otherwise would be neglected The near-invisibility of practical intentionality has led to a blindness in relation to the full range of layers that constitute the decision-making process.[6] Since practical intentionality does not belong fully to either passive or active intentionality, it can easily be neglected. This means that practical intentionality does not equate with the active decisions we make when we resolve ourselves to a specific direction, neither is it the passive flow in which we stay when we live our lives without being aware of what we are doing; instead, practical intentionality points to that moment of awakening in which we are aware of our body and our self as standing in this flow and decide to validate or not our next move toward a new specific direction. Moreover, from a theoretical point of view, I think that practical intentionality allows us to make visible the wide range of intentional acts mentioned by Husserl in his research.[7]

Second, as Bernet noted in his introduction to *Analyses Concerning Passive and Active Syntheses*: "intentionality is not a structure that stems one-sidedly from consciousness; it is a dynamic cooperative structure, a constitutive duet" (iii; cf. 52). Looking at intentionality only from an active perspective distorts our ability to describe a phenomenon, for the phenomenon arises from an active and passive determination of matter. Similar to Husserl's notion of the double apriori (*doppelte Apriori*, Hua XXXII, 120),[8] intentionality cannot be conceived of only from its formal side. Rather, it also must be seen from its dynamic and practical side; in fact its practical side provides the clue to explain the dynamic cooperative relationship between active and passive intentionality.[9] In particular when we examine love we cannot look at the phenomenon of caring for someone from the perspective of the active intentions taken by the subject, because care (as well as many other faces of love) manifests itself through small passive acts that reveal the actual intention of the agent.

Third, I think that an increased focus on practical intentionality would give phenomenologists greater access to the realm of Praxis tout court, for example, "*Denkpraxis*," (Hua XLII, 361) or "*Geltung Praxis*," (Hua XXXIX, 1).[10] Practical aiming is as important as theoretical aiming in disclosing the realm of lived-experiences. Valuing, as much as thinking, is a form of reasoning that aims at matter in a constitutive way. In *Logical Investigations* (1901) Husserl writes:

> The term intention hits off the peculiarity of acts by imagining them to aim at something and so fits the numerous cases that are naturally and understandably ranked as cases of theoretical and *practical aiming*. In talking of acts, on the other hand, we must steer clear of the word's original meaning: all thought of activity must be rigidly excluded.[11]

Practisches Abzielen (practical reference) does not refer to a natural action; instead, it refers to a practical aiming at—a being consciousness of—that Husserl explains as intentionality in the mode of wakefulness (Hua XLII, 51).

Therefore in what follows I will refer primarily to the *Logical Investigations* (1901), *Ideas* (1983/1913), and the *Analyses Concerning Passive and Active Synthesis* (2001/1859–1938) in order to describe the evolution of Husserl's thought in relation to the issue of intentionality. This analysis is aimed at providing the theoretical foundations for the phenomenological research that I will pursue in the following chapters.

In what follows I will explain why I consider the insight of practical intentions (Hua VIII, 34) as being already present in Husserl's writings of 1901, but only later, with the introduction of the genetic method, fully explicated as the meaning of "practical" intentions.[12] In the first part of this chapter I will describe what Husserl means by "intentions." In the second part I will consider Husserl's analysis of intentionality in the *Logical Investigations*, *Ideas* and the *Analyses*. Through the examination of this latter, I will explore one specific declension of practical intentionality; namely, affective intentionality.

Intention

I will first seek to describe the constituents of an intentional act and show how intentional activities differ from all forms of natural action. In so doing I will comment on three passages representing three different periods of Husserl's writing on intentionality and which, taken together, cover the arc of his philosophical career.

In *Logical Investigations* (1901) Husserl describes intention as "a theoretical and practical aiming at" from which "all thought of activity must be rigidly excluded."[13] Intention cannot be confused with action, for it is not equivalent to the natural attitude that we inhabit when we are living spontaneously. Instead, intention is a practical and theoretical *aiming at (Beziehung auf)* something that seems to transcend us. For this reason in Greek tradition intentionality has been defined as a *paron apon* (a present absence). When I reflect upon my own intentional acts I set aside the object that is outside of me in order to attend to the object as it is held in my consciousness, an object that no longer possesses the ontological structure of a transcendent object. The meant (intended) object is present to me, but ontologically absent at the same time: a *paron apon*. For this reason intentionality cannot indicate a mere activity: it attends to the existence of the object not within a natural flow of activities, but rather through a reflective aiming at them. As its Latin etymology indicates, *reflection* implies a bending (*flector*) back (*re-*) to what has already been lived, and as Husserl wrote, this bending back can be theoretical or practical. Theoretically we can think of something in a reflective way; practically we can feel something in an aware way.[14] I can theoretically decide to get closer to a person, but practically I feel held back. In this case I can engage a theoretical and practical reflection in order to understand why I live in such contrast and it might be that the practical reflection would bring to an answer that is much more reliable than the cognitive one. Unfortunately, today the term reflection is commonly understood in an almost exclusively cognitive sense, which is neglectful of the fact that for ages human beings sought to pursue a form of practical reflection named wisdom or *sophia* which was held to transcend the cognitive and to comprehend the cognitive into the practical.

Husserl's characterization of intention in *Ideas I* (1983/1913) does not differ significantly from *Logical Investigations*. In *Ideas* intention is described as "seizing upon (…), objectifying turn, <for example> being turned valuingly to a thing involves (…) a seizing upon the mere thing; not the mere thing but rather the valuable thing" (Hua III, 66). Similarly to the *Logical Investigations*, what makes intention an intention in the *Ideas* is the reflective attitude through which we objectify what appears to us. Intention indicates the ability of consciousness to transform undifferentiated matter into a unit of meaning. In the lines just cited from *Ideas*, the practical seizing of sensuous data is explained through valuing activity.

Finally, in the *Anaylses* (1859–1938) Husserl describes intention in the following terms:

> Intention is (…) a presenting endeavor that wants to realize itself in the continuous acquisition of knowledge, in a fulfilling grasp of the self that is constantly in the process of determining more closely, that is, not just in a mere grasping of the self in general, but rather being interfused, with an endeavor into the moments of the object and to see to what extent they are not yet intuitively realized as grasping the self, in order to bring them to this realization.
>
> *(Hua XL, 85)*

In the preceding analysis Husserl's phenomenological description is strongly influenced by his genetic method. Objectivation is described as an ongoing process that involves the self's efforts to aim at the moments that make the object different from the self. The "endeavour" refers to the ongoing process of differentiation of the self from matter through affections and awakening. In its natural attitude the self is undifferentiated matter. It becomes an egoic self when, affected by matter, the ego awakes and takes a position in relation to the matter while simultaneously giving it a sense. The awakening yields a form of primordial validation, a practical reflection through which consciousness objectifies itself (Hua XL, 221, 277).

This brief analysis of three passages demonstrates that for Husserl the essence of intention lies in its ability to aim at. By "aiming at" Husserl means the capacity to objectivate sensuous data in an intentional unit of sense; that is, to bring the content to its realization by an awake ego. Now let us more closely examine the meaning of intentional essence in the *Logical Investigations*, *Ideas*, and *Analyses*.

Intentional Essence in Logical Investigations

In the first section of the fifth *Logical Investigation* Husserl defines consciousness as "a comprehensive designation for 'mental acts' or 'intentional experiences' of all sorts" (Hua XIX, 346; En. 81). He dedicates the following sections to explaining what intentional acts are and what makes them intentional. From sections 20 to 22 he describes the essence of intentional acts meant not as acts in which "we live" (Hua XIX, 411; En. tr. 119) but as the phenomena that appear to us when we reflect on them. An intentional essence is that which makes an act an objectifying one; that is, an act in which the object is presented to us.

The primary structure of an intentional essence is comprised of a correlation of matter and quality. They are unthinkable separately (Hua XIX, 416; En. tr. 122) because quality is the way in which matter presents itself, while matter is that which the quality presents.

Yet, "the intentional essence does not exhaust the act phenomeno-logically" (Hua XIX, 416; En. tr. 123). We could not speak about intentional essences if "the fullness or vividness of the sensuous contents" (Hua XIX, 415; En. tr. 121) did not help to "build" the act. It is this fullness that stimulates the act of apprehension (*Aufassung*) and therefore the intentional act. For example, when one feels attraction for another person the matter of one's body presents itself in a way that stimulates the natural desire to be with that other body. This material desire might constitute the basis for an actual act of pursuing the other in an intentional way.

In the fifth *Logical Investigation* section 11–20 Husserl describes the non-intentional matter as initiating the process of determination, while intentional matter determines how the content of an act will be constituted according to its quality. In *Logical Investigations* the intentional act is intentional because it is an objectifying act. The combination of quality and matter is such that intentional matter founds the quality that determines the content in a specific way (Hua XIX, V, section 23). Nevertheless, it is non-intentional matter, or fullness that triggers the reference to an object in the natural attitude. This fullness makes the sensuous object a *meant object* and its matter a *represented matter*. Following up on the example given above, it is the physical attraction, that is the non-intentional sensuous matter, that calls for its own determination, that is the constitution of a practical or cognitive meaning (I will spend time with that person or I know I like that person). The relationship between non-intentional and intentional matter is observed in the dynamic co-operation of active and passive intentions.

Intentional Essence in Ideas

While in *Logical Investigations* (1901) the intentional essence was defined as the correlation of matter and form, which was in turn animated by fullness (or non-intentional matter), in *Ideas I* (1983/1913) Husserl describes intentionality through the noetic–noematic correlation as animated by the synolon hyle-morphe.

As in the *Logical Investigations*, intentionality is "a comprehensive name for all inclusive phenomenological structures (...) Under intentionality we understand the own peculiarity of mental processes to be conscious of something" (Hua III, 168). Intentionality indicates the effort to be conscious of the content of our lived-experience. When Husserl indicates intentionality as an act in which consciousness becomes consciousness of something, he refers to the act through which the consciousness becomes spirit, reason, or soul; that is, *the act through which undifferentiated data acquire its sense as a whole.*

In *Thing and Space* (1973) Husserl describes the genesis of the noema as a system of strata grouped around a central core or around an objective sense (Hua XVI, 222, section 89).

The givenness of the object appears as a self-presenting (*Selbst-stellend*) object.

The appearance of the thing occurs in two layers: first, we have the space-form, filled with *Empfidungen* (sensuous qualities) associated with each other in accordance with kinesthetic lawfulness (Hua XVI, sections 72–73), the temporal schema. This schema orders appearances in a system of retentions and protentions (Hua XVI, section 80) to which is attached a sensuous fullness that fills the form of the appearance with its matter according to the apriori possibilities that the kinetic determination of that object requires (Hua XVI, section 38). The second layer may be called the layer of causal properties and is concerned with substantial-causal reality. This second level of *res materialis* bridges to the first layer and interprets the non-intentional matter of the first layer (the appearance of that object) according to a specific genus. Applying this description on the example I provided above, the givenness of the body of another person is such that one might perceive in a moment in time the smell of that body, its shape, its hormonal balance and so forth. All that sensuous matter is organized by our brain according to a specific shape and form to which we assign a meaning. This meaning can vary according to the level of awareness one reached with that matter. In general, the number of sensuous data perceived constitute a material core that calls for qualities that we determine through an infinite array of meanings.

In sections 95–100 Husserl describes the constitution of noematic strata.[15] Once reduced, the sensuous data can become components of the complete mental process of intentive functions because "they present themselves as stuffs or intentive formings, or sense-bestowings belonging to different levels" (Hua XVI, section 85; in particular page 203 of the English translation). The layers of the noema and its noetic correlates depend upon the level of these intentive formations. Layers will be simpler or more complex according to the kind of objectivation, ordered by eidetically lawful hierarchical foundations (Hua XVI, sections 100–113).

"The sensuousness – which comprises feelings and drives have their own unity" (Hua XVI, 205). "The experienced physical thing proper provides the mere "This," an empty X which becomes the bearer of (…) determinations." Indeed, this index or empty X calls for data that subordinate one to the other and create a unity of sensuousness that wraps around that call. Then as scientists we reduce and determine this unit in a functional interpretation.[16]

Gefühlsintentionalität

On the basis of the analysis conducted above, two main characteristics emerge as essential for an intentional act. First, an act is intentional if it reflects on the sensuous data (non-intentional matter) that are experienced in a natural attitude. Second, an act is intentional if while aiming at these sensuous data it constitutes them as a meaningful whole. In the following section I will address Husserl's definition of "feeling," or affective intentionality, in order to establish whether this form of intentionality satisfies these two characteristics, and in order to shed light on the role played by practical intentions in affective intentional activity.

Affection and Passivity

The English volume that collects the writings on *Analyses Concerning Passive and Active Syntheses* proves that genetic and static phenomenology, and passive and active intentionality, were complementary from the very beginning of Husserl's phenomenological research. The volume collects texts written between 1859 and 1939. In the book Husserl mentions a variety of forms of intentionality—hidden (21), affective (281), feeling (278), latent (22, 371)—that cannot be technically assimilated to the kind of intentionality that he mentions in *Logical Investigations* or *Ideas*.

We know that Husserl examined the intentionality of feelings and sentiments early in his career in section 15 of the V *Logical Investigations*;[17] at that time the position he took was highly influenced by his two teachers, Stumpf and Brentano. However in the *Analyses* (section 50, part 3) he revisited his analysis of feelings in much greater detail. Importantly, in the *Analyses* he seems to state that feeling intentionality has an objectivating character.

His first argumentative move in the *Analyses* is to explain how passivity relates to intentionality, in particular to the intentionality of feeling. "Passivity (…) means here the mode of intentionality of feeling without active egoic participation and the corresponding active mode" (Hua XXXI, 8). In this passage passivity is a mode of practical intentionality because it indicates the in-between space in which the non-ego becomes an ego. In this in-between space the ego has not taken yet a position in relation to non-intentional matter because it has just been awoken in response to matter and called by it to predicative activity. Affection awakens the ego while it is still in a condition of dormant matter. As Husserl writes in *Cartesian Meditations*:

> the Ego that in any sense is *"active"* and *takes a position* (…) is only one side. Opposed to the active Ego stands the passive, and the Ego is always *passive* at the same time whenever it is active, in the sense of being affected as well as being receptive, which of course does not exclude possibility of its being sheer passivity.
>
> *(Hua I, 224–225)*

It is impossible to think of the ego as always being an active subject because insofar as it lives in a natural attitude, the matter with which it interacts and of which it is part has not yet been objectivated. While one is spending time with their partner, a number of sensuous experiences can take place of which one is not fully aware—hunger, fear, intense sense of intimacy, etc. (this is what I am going to explore in the next chapters). In these experiences the ego is not fully awake, but rather is driven by a flow of matter. The active ego stands only in the choice that that person made to spend its time with her partner—that time is the only intentional meaning emerging from the given experience.

Intentionality cannot be reduced to the active process of an ego-act that objectivates sensuous data, because it also involves the process of objectivating the ego from not-yet-egoic matter. It is the intentionality of feeling that awakens the ego and allows it to objectify itself and its contents. *The form of objectivation that belongs to practical intentionality refers to the passive ego that, once awake, reflects upon its matter and objectivates itself as a meaningful subject.*[18] As I will discuss in the following chapters, this form of intentionality has relevant consequences on the analysis of love, sex, and intimate life.

In fact, the source from which this form of intentionality stems is called affection. "Already within passivity affection is a specific modality of objectivation for the ego" (Hua XXXI, 8) that is first directed toward the ego and then toward its contents. It represents a form of primordial objectivation. For Husserl, while primordial association is independent of the ego, it awakens the ego. At first the necessary lawfulness of given data is recognized by an egoless affection; then this egoless affection secures the given data within a system of interrelated data, while awakening the structure of something different from and yet relating to the data.

The awakening of the ego as a meaningful and aware unit is the first form of objectivation through which undifferentiated matter is given to the just-born subject as a whole.

According to this description the structure of fulfillment of pure objectivation is such that (Hua XL, 65–121) affection as a primordial impression exerts a force (Hua XXXI, 477–478, XI, 173) on the subject who is called in time—that is, through a chain of protentions and retentions—to accept or deny the legitimacy of the arising presenta-tion.[19] In the living moment of that original impression the subject originally makes present the validation of always-new appearances.[20] The validations as

> values determinations are not the arbitrarily varying characters of feeling, they are predicates, that is, elements that are identifiable; but the sources from which the objectivation for these predicates are drawn are the feelings and the contents of them accruing to the matters in questions.
>
> *(Hua XXXI, 8)*

Thus, feeling is a primordial form of attributing meaning to a given sen-suous matter. Being in contact with one's feeling can trigger the first layer of objectivation by which we determine the sense of our matter.

"The object is constituted in and through the objectivating that underlines the intentionality of feeling, and is progressively constituted in a distinctive path of identifications," (Hua XXXI, 6). Feeling inten-tionality represents a primordial form of objectivation that seems to originate from affect-consciousness (*Gemütbewusstsein*, Hua XXXI, 5) and is addressed to the constitution of the ego and its practical, as well as formal, reflections.[21] While in *Ideas* and *Logical Investigations* Husserl attributed the role of triggering intentional aiming to non-intentional matter or hyle, in the *Analyses* he seems to attribute an objectivating character to the interaction between hyle and affection. Non-intentional matter seems to demonstrate an intentional quality, although in a purely practical way. As the morning star would not change if I called it by a different name, similarly killing someone would not be right if a govern-ment gave me allowance to do it. It is thanks to this reflection that we are able to reflect on sensuous matter, practically or theoretically, in a way that is intentional, meaning that is not naïve and cannot be assimilated to my natural experience of it.

Practical intentionality involves the capacity to reflect on lived-experience through awareness and wakefulness: this form of objectivation is described by Husserl as a form of awakening[22]—"intentionality in the mode of wakefulness."[23]

Conclusion

This chapter examined the characteristics of intentional acts (i.e., objectivating and reflective aiming at) and how these characteristics apply to the practical component of intentional acts with the goal of displaying the theoretical foundations of the research I will conduct in the following chapters. While in *Logical Investigations* non-intentional matter seems to be neatly distinguished from intentional matter, in *Ideas* and in the *Analyses* non-intentional matter seems to constitute a bridge for matter to become intentional and constitutive of meaning. In the *Analyses* feeling intentionality is not only that which triggers an intention; it is also an objectivating force. Hence feeling intentionality, which will be central in the analysis of love, intimate, and sexual life that I will conduct in the coming chapters, is an invisible layer of the intentional structure that should not remain invisible to the eyes of the phenomenologist who wants to investigate the life of the heart; this layer, in fact, represents a primordial form of objectivation that originates from affect-consciousness (*Gemütbewusstsein*, Hua XXXI, 5) and fulfills itself in the constitution of the ego. This form of objectivation awakens an ego that, as a subject of acts, can reflect in an awake way upon its content-matter and distinguish itself from them in a way that constitutes itself as a meaningful whole. The primordiality of matter is not intentional in itself when it acts as the trigger for further objectivation; however, matter is intentional in the validating and affective process through which it awakens the ego and leads it to objectivate itself and its contents. Within this primordiality there is a thin intentional layer that calls for practical reflection and the constitution of meaning; this layer is what I have called—with Husserl's permission—*practical intention*; that is, the intentionality of consciousness in the mode of wakefulness (Hua XLII, 51).

Notes

1 Here I am using the translation that James Hart used in his *Person and Common Life*.

2 See for example Steinbock's analyses of the evidence of the heart (*Moral Emotions*) or James Hart's *The Person and the Common Life*.
3 See for example: Hua XXVIII, XXXVII, Hua-Mat VIII, Hua XXXIX, text 1.
4 Practical intentionality is also addressed by Husserl in manuscript A VII 13, A IV 9 and in Hua VIII, 34, XI, 61, XIV, 172. For the intention of willing and practical reason see Hua VIII, 230, 201, 203.
5 Hua VII, 34:

> Im erkennenden Handeln die praktische Intention durch blosse Seinsmeinung zur Selbsthabe des gemeinten Seins hinstrebt und das es in der Tat jeweils so etwas gibt oder geben kann wie Evidenz, und Evidenz verschiedener Stufen, bis zum Limes der Adäquation—als Voraussetzung für die entsprechende Gradualität der Befriedigung des erkennenden Strebens?

6 Also, it leads to an unfortunate interpretation of Husserl as a narrowly Cartesian and intellectualist philosopher.
7 I am referring to for example, instinctive intentionality, vertical, longitudinal (Hua XXX), collective (Hua XIV), intersubjective, social, affective, (cf., e.g., Hua XIV, 196ff. and Husserl 1923), vitally flowing intentionality (lebendig strömende Intentionalität) (Hua VI, 259), intentional will (*Willensintention* or *Willensmeinung*) (Hua XXVIII, XXXVII).
8 See: Hua XXXVII, 24, 220, 232, 268, 269, 265, 227, 266, 411ff., 223; Hua XXXI, 8, 267; Hua XXVIII, 414, 402f. As it concerns his notion of apriori in relation to Kant (Hua XXVII, 255; Hua XXVIII, 244; Hua XIX, 260; Hua XVII, 390–402; Hua XXXVII, 221–226) and to Hume's relation of ideas (Hua VII, 235; Hua XIX/1, B1, 439).
9 On this note it is not a surprise that Biceaga speaks about objectifying passivity (2010, 22).
10 Hua XXXIX, 382–383: "Sprachliche Praxis, Praxis der Erzeugung objektiver Wahrheiten, eine Urteilspraxis, die auf ideale Gebilde geht in Bezug auf Reales und zunächst auf Verkörperlichungen des Idealen. Also der Titel Erkenntnis: Das sind Formen der Praxis (...)."
  Hua XXXIX, 383: "Praxis ist die Unterlage der realen (...) Praxis des Wahrnehmens (...) leibliche Praxis, in denen die Bestimmungen des Dinges selbst in Vollkommenheitsstufen sichtlich werden."
11 Emphasis mine, Hua XIX, 358:

> Der Ausdruck Intention stellt die Eigenheit der Acte unter dem. Bilde des Abzielens vor und pafst daher sehr gut auf die mannigfaltigen Acte, die sich ungezwungen und allgemein.verständlich *als theoretisches oder practisches Abzielen* bezeichnen lassen. (…) Was andererseits die Rede von Acten anbelangt, so darf man hier an den ursprünglichen Wortsinn von actus natürlich nicht mehr denken, der Gedanke der Bethätigung mufs schlechterdings ausgeschlossen bleiben.

12 On the continuity between static and genetic phenomenology see for example Leask, I. (2011) and Jacques Derrida, "'Genesis and Structure' and 'Phenomenology,'" in *Writing and Difference*, (trans. Bass, A., London: Routledge & Kegan Paul, 1978), 154–168, 165; "Genèse et structure et la phénoménologie de Husserl," in *L'Ecriture et la différence* (Paris: Editions du Seuil, 1967), 229–251, 248.

13 Der Ausdruck Intention stellt die Eigenheit der Acte unter dem. Bilde des Abzielens vor und pafst daher sehr gut auf die mannigfaltigen Acte, die sich ungezwungen und allgemein.verständlich als theoretisches oder practisches Abzielen bezeichnen lassen. (…) Was andererseits die Rede von Acten anbelangt, so darf man hier an den ursprünglichen Wortsinn von actus natürlich nicht mehr denken, der Gedanke der Bethätigung mufs schlechterdings ausgeschlossen bleiben. (1901), 358.

14 Hua XLII, 243–244: "Vor der Reflexion ist dabei schon wache Ich in einem ausgezeichneten Modus, einem Urmodus aktiv: wach aktiv. Und das wird in diesem Modus reflexive thematisch, wieder in einem Wach-Akt."

15 There is a voluminous literature and heated debate regarding the noetic-noematic correlation. We can divide the literature into two main groups, the intensional and intentional literature. This latter can still be broken down into two other groups, one which interprets the foundation as directionality from *concretum* to *abstractum*, and vice-versa instead for the other. Føllesdal emphasizes the intensional character of the noema. Indeed, he considers the noema as an *abstractum* founded in the *concretum; the noema* is the generalization of meaning. On this same line, Smith and McIntyre's celebrated interpretation regards the noema as an intentional content, ontologically distinct from the object (meant as intended object). According to the intensional interpretation, the noema is the content of the object and not the real object (Hua XIX, V, 20–22). It bears a relational or referential character that depends on the meanings and is always expressed through language. Gurtwisch's position can be ascribed to the second interpretive group. In fact, he considers the noema as "an incarnate meaning" (Gurtiwisch, 1974). The noema is interpreted as the immediate correlate of perceptual consciousness. The noema cannot be the physical object because the physical object appears to us in many different moments; neither can the ideal entity be correlated to any moment of perception (although it is not ontologically distinct from moments of perception), because otherwise the ideal entity would lack of its unitarity. The noema is a complex of momentary noemata. For Dreyfus the noema is the reference, that is, the ideal object in its relation to a fulfillment. Differently from both Gurwitsch and Smith & McIntyre, the noema is not sense because sense is empty. Instead, the noema is a pure referential bridge between a given sense and its appearances. Finally, Drummond, commenting critically on the preceding literature, proposes we think of the noema and the outer object not as a whole-part structure but rather as an identity-in-manifolds analysis. In other words he considers the noema and the object as ontologically and

epistemologically separated from each other. "Thus, identity-in-manifolds analysis cannot be reduced to whole/parts analysis as Gurwitsch argues" (Drummond, 1990, 151). Drummond following on Gurwitsch proposes that the relationship between the noema and the outer object be interpreted as a relationship between *abstractum* and *concretum*, but differently from Gurwitsch he separates this structure from the theory of parts and whole. For Drummond it is only in the abstractum/concretum relationship that we can properly grasp the dynamism and simultaneity of the perceptual process.

16 There is "a unity of construing (...) grounded in the essence of those construings, to make up a unity of construings, grounded in the essence of various unities of construing" (Hua XVI, 41; in particular page 88 of the English translation). See also:

> It must be borne clearly in mind that the Data of sensation which exercise the function of adumbrations of color, of smoothness, of shape, etc. (the function of presentation) are, of essential necessity, entirely different from color simpliciter, smoothness simpliciter, shaper simpliciter, and, in short, form all kinds of moments belonging to the physical things. The adumbrations, though called by the same name, of essential necessity is not of the same genus as the one to which the adumbrated belongs. The adumbrating is a mental process.
>
> *(Hua XVI, 41; En. tr. 88)*

17 As Fisette (2009) remarked, Husserl is taking a position in the long-standing debate between Stumpf and Brentano that began in 1899 and ended with Brentano's death in 1916. The main terms of this debate can be summarized in the following way: according to Brentano there are three categories of acts: representations, judgments, and sentiments. Brentano considers emotions as acts that are different from sensory feelings. In fact, according to Brentano sensory feelings can trigger emotions but are not themselves emotions. Emotions are, like sentiments of hate and love, a high level of acts which are based on representation and affect the representation with a *Mitempfindung*, that is, a feeling of pleasure or pain. Stumpf does not share this position. He divides phenomena into two main groups: intellectual functions (perception, representations and judgments) and affective functions (emotions, desires and will). Under the affective functions he groups sense-feelings and in particular anhedonic feelings. There are people who can no longer feel pleasure while doing things that used to give them pleasure. Husserl, being a disciple of both Brentano and Stumpf, seems to have taken an intermediate position in this debate. Indeed, in his fifth *Logical Investigation* he states that, differently from what Brentano claimed, pain and pleasure are not intentional because, as stated by Stumpf, they are sensory qualities. Yet, to a certain extent, emotions are intentional because, as Brentano remarked, some emotions can be animated by sensory feelings. According to Husserl we can refer to objects that are representable for us through the representations that are interwoven with those

objects. Sentiments are not intentional because we do not have a real object to sense. Sentiments are not given as a whole because of the representations with which they are interwoven. "They are not acts <intentional acts>, but are constituted through them" (Hua XIX, 390; En. tr. 109).

18 On this point it is interesting to read also Husserl's Bernau Manuscript, text 14–15 in which the I is ultimately presented as object-I, objectified through reflection. The reflection envisioned here has nothing to do with thoughts, since it is mostly related to the primordial matter and time both appearing in the form of stream of consciousness. See also on this point Lohmar, D. and Yamaguchi, I. *On Time.*

19 Hua XI, 173:

> We encounter an entirely peculiar affective accomplishment within the living present, namely, the accomplishment of awakening the (…) element shrouded in implicit intentionality. So long as the new force lasts, the objectlike moments that have attained a special affection are affectively preserved in the empty form of presentation, thus sustained longer than without this new force.

20 Hua XI, 37:

> Under the given intentional situation, modified or completely new sense-data that arise demand precisely [those] apprehensions that complete the remaining uncontested intentions; they demand the apprehensions to complete the intentions in such a way that the source of the contention is quelled, and what is especially motivating the doubt will be annulled through the force of a primordial impression. Fulfillment through a primordial impression is the force that mows everything down. We move closer to it, we clasp it with our hand, touching it, and the dubious intention of wax we just had gets the priority of certainty. It gets this through the concordant transition to new appearances that do not accord with the apprehension of human being and its unfulfilled horizons, and negates the latter through its fulfilling weight of being presented in the flesh. With respect to the one instance, a negation takes place in this decision; in particular, it takes place with respect to the apprehension of human being that is guiding the original perception and that then becomes modalized as dubious. In the opposite case, an affirmation would have occurred, or what amounts to the same thing, a ratification of the original perception, but which later became dubious. That which appeared in the flesh would have then received the modal validity character of "yes, really." So, in a certain respect even the ratifying Yes, like the No, is a mode of modifying certain validity and is distinct from the entirely original "entirely unmodified mode of certain validity; the straightforward constitution of the perceptual object is carried out univocally in this mode, and without struggle.

21 Hua XLII, 241: "Das Gemüt und der Wille sind eine eigene Quelle des Rechten und Echte; und das Urteil kommt nur nach, es zu erfassen und zu konstatieren. Und das Gemüt ist eine eigene Quelle auch für den Seinsglauben."

22 Hua XVII, 362: "We arrive at both these types in their contrast by presentifying actual lived-experiences of awakening, by a retrospective intuitive grasping of preceding phases of consciousness in comparison with wakefulness itself."

23 See on this: Hua XLII, 51:

Aktinentionalität im Modus der Wacheheit. (…) 'Selbstvergessen' bin ich insofern, als ich nicht auf mich und mein Fungieren reflektiv gerichtet bin, was wieder ein Wachakt wäre, gerichtet auf mein subjektives gegenwärtiges Sein und Leben. Vor der Reflexion ist dabei schon wache Ich in einem ausgezeichneten Modus, einem Urmodus aktiv: wach aktiv. Und das wird in diesem Modus reflexive thematisch, wieder in einem Wach-Akt;

Hua XLII, 243–244:

Alle Intentionalität, also aller Stufen, hat die Form "Trieb." Zunächst passiv sich auslebender, bald ungehemmt sich erfüllender oder gehemmter Trieb. In hörerer Stufe, in der Modalität, die ihr zugehört, Wachweden des Ich für die im passive Trieb und eines erfüllten oder auch eines unerfüllten Triebes, also auch davon affiziert; and

Hua XLII, 244:

In der Auswirkung der Triebe in Form wacher, ichzentrierter Intentionalität kostituieren sich für das Ich seiende Einheiten und seiend in Stufen der Bedeusamkeit mit einem Kern, der unserer blossen Natur entsprechen muss. Aus der intentionalen Analyse der Sinngebung und der Sinngestalten der verschiedenen sich aufeinander studenden und verflechtendedn Grundarten der Intentionalität wird sie Struktur der Triebe und Vermögen korrelativ verständlich.

Bibliography

Bernet, R. (1994). *La vie du Sujet. Recherches sur l'interprétation de Husserl dans la Phénoménologie*. Paris: P. U. F.

Crowell, S. (2013). *Normativity and Phenomenology in Husserl and Heidegger*. Cambridge: Cambridge University Press.

Drummond, J. J. (1990). *Husserlian Intentionality and Non-Foundational Realism: Noema and Objects*. Boston: Kluwer Academic Publishers.

Ferrarello, S. (2015). *Husserl's Ethics and Practical Intentionality*. London/New York: Bloomsbury.

Fisette, D. (2009). "Love and Hate: Brentano and Stumpf on Emotions and Sense Feelings." *Gestalt Theorie*, vol. 31, no. 2, 115–127.

Gurwitsch, A. (1974). *Phenomenology and the Theory of Science*, Evanston: Northwestern University.

Hart, J. (1998). *Person and Common Life,* Dordrecht/Boston/London: Kluwer Academic Publishers.

Husserl, E. (1901). *Logical Investigations*, (trans. Findlay, J. N. and ed. Moran, D.). London and New York: Routledge.

Husserl, E. (1973). *Ding und Raum,* (ed. Claesges, U). The Hague, Netherlands: Martinus Nijhoff.

Husserl, E. (1983/1913). (Husserliana III) *Ideas Pertaining to a Pure Phenomenology and to a Phenomenological Philosophy*, (ed. Kersten, F.). The Hague: Martinus Nijhoff.

Husserl, E. (1989). *Ideas Pertaining to a Pure Phenomenology and to a Phenomenological Philosophy, Second Book*, (trans. Rojcewicz, R. and Schuwer, A.). Dordrecht: Kluwer Academic Publishers.

Husserl, E. (1989). *Cartesian Meditations*, (trans. Cairns, D.). Dordrecht: Kluwer Academic Publishers.

Husserl, E. (2001/1859–1938). *Analyses Concerning Passive and Active Syntheses. Lectures on Transcendental Logic*, (trans. Steinbock, A. J.). Dordrecht: Kluwer Academic Publishers.

Husserl, E. (2001). *Logical Investigations*, (trans. Findlay, J. N. and ed. Moran, D.). London and New York: Routledge.

Lee, N. (2000). "Practical Intentionality and Transcendental Phenomenology as a Practical Philosophy." *Husserl Studies* vol. 17, 49–63.

Lohmar, D. and Yamaguchi, I. (2010). *On Time. New Contributions on the Husserlian Phenomenology of Time.* Dordrecht-Heidelberg-London-New York: Kluwer Academic Publishers.

Steinbock, A. (2014). *Moral Emotions.* Evanston: Northwestern University Press.

2

SEX WITH AND WITHOUT THE EGO

Introduction

Sex—we love it, we hate it; it scares us, it makes all our problems disappear; we never do it enough, we are not good at it. There is so much to say on this topic that any beginning seems hopeless. Traditional Western philosophy, from Plato to Marx, seems to grant to sex a propellive energy capable to drive massive social and political change in human life, more often male human life (Dickinson, 2002). On my part, what I am interested to explore in this chapter is what we mean by sexual life, what are its layers and accordingly the meanings that describe sexuality, especially in what relates to the ego.

In doing so I will discuss Husserl's view of sexuality as he reflects on it in his pages on intersubjectivity (Hua XV) and on intentionality of copulation (Hua XV, 596). For this reason, I propose to investigate the relationship between practical intentionality, and intentionality of copulation in relation to Husserl's notion of operating and not-operating will, desires and instincts. Hence, the chapter is divided into three parts. First, the analysis of will and its egoic and egoless functions; second, the analysis of desires and instincts as they form habits and beliefs; finally the analysis of egoless intentionality and sex.

Willing

It is often the case that what moves our sexual choices in life is our will more than our cognitive reason; often the two forms of reason are not even capable of communicating with each other. Our cognitive reason cannot be always convinced about the rightness of the decisions made by our sensuous will. If an easy dialogue between the two were possible, women would be more likely to not have children and love would have been extinguished a long time ago seeing how frightening the two experiences might be. Hence, in order to describe our sexual lives I will begin with the faculty that I believe predominantly moves our choices in the matter of sex: our will, in its passive and active, egoless and egoic forms.

Operating and Not-Operating Willing

In his lectures on ethics and value theory (1914) Husserl writes that:

> The will (...) takes part in the more general sphere of pure reason (...) the specific and pregnant meaning of will refers solely to a particular kind of activity that underpins all the other fields of consciousness (...). It seems even more evident that the will (...) is a particular and superior form of activity that can come into play everywhere under some essential conditions that lie in objectivations and in presupposed sentiments.
> *(Husserl XXXVIII, 68; Cf. also Hua XXXI, 9–10)*

As this passage shows, willing is not something different from reason, rather it is a big part of our rationality; without willing our rational choices would be empty and motionless, without thinking our willings would be chaotic and invisible to us. According to Husserl, willing is the practical motivational force underlying any conscious field. As a subjective faculty it properly belongs to the higher spiritual level, although it can be activated only from the lower spiritual layer. I will say more on higher and lower spiritual level in Chapter 4; here it suffices to say that by "lower" Husserl means the egoless spiritual level that pertains to instincts, impulses, affections; and he refers to the egoic spiritual level that relates to motivations, thoughts, and higher feelings as "higher." While the lower level does not involve any position taken by the ego and it involves the passive life of the body, the higher level calls for a position that the ego has to take in relation to the direction that it wants to give to its body.

To describe the passage from lower to higher spiritual level, Husserl distinguishes three forms of willing acts: the resolve (*Vorsatz*), the *fiat*, and the action-will (*Handlungswille*).[1] I will describe the first two in the next sections. The third one, action-will, can be further distinguished into operating and not-operating willing (Hua XXVIII, 118). Operating will is a form of procedural willing that does not yet know what it is about to decide, but is directed toward the accomplishment of a goal. The not-operating will is at work when my I is just emerging from the realm of passivity and becoming a subject. In the example given before, I notice that *my* eyes are intent on my partner and realize that I feel attracted to him now. Only after that awakening does the not-operating will become an operating one in which my I is aware of the goal that my living body wants to achieve, (Hua XXVIII, 118), following the example "I want to go home."

Practical possibilities always relate to a subject who can want them (Hua XXVIII, 122). Tendency, attention, and interest are the three movements of the soul that explicate the transition from a not-operating to an operating will, from a lower spiritual level to a higher one. Initially, as stated before, the I is just receptive.

> In receptivity, although the ego is indeed actively turned toward what affects it, it does not make its knowledge, and the individual steps of cognition (...) an object of will.
>
> *(Husserl, 1973, 198)*

The receptive activity creates a horizon of apprehending attention that modifies the structure of the not-yet-I, into a tension, meaning the I *tendens ad* (stretching toward) its object:

> In general, *attention* is a tending of the ego toward an intentional object, toward a unity which appears continually in the change of the modes of its givens (...); it is a tending toward realization.
>
> *(Husserl, 1973, 80)*

As is shown in the quotation, attention is a physical tension that can be accepted or denied by the subject who is aware of it. This kind of physical tension is the main component of the intentionality of coitus that will be described in more detail in the next sections; it is this form of intentionality that explains the bridge between lower to higher spiritual level—what Husserl called "the resolve" and "the fiat" of the "operating will" from the "not-operating one." In this tension the sexual instincts move from a blind egoless and not-operating will toward an egoic realization. Indeed, if the egoless tension is accepted and then enhanced by the I that tension becomes interest; the interest (*dabei sein*) allows the I to actually participate in that object and transform the act of tension into an act of apprehension.[2] The will is operating in the objectifying act; that is, in the attempt to grasp its object and fix its predicative and practical sense once and for all.

> When we distinguish two levels of interest and, corresponding to these, two levels of objectifying operations, viz. that belonging to receptive experience, on the one hand, and that of predicative spontaneity, on the other, this distinction of levels should not be construed as if the different operations were somehow separate from each other.
>
> *(Husserl, 1973, 203)*

The transition from the lower to the higher spirit is mediated by the ongoing interplay of two levels of spiritual operations, a receptive and a predicative one—sexual instincts become sexual active choices through this transition.

Doxic and Axiological Will

According to this two-layered structure, volitions are first founded upon emotional consciousness (in Husserl's terms, *Gemüt*, a word that indicates more than the solely emotional and comprehends the axiological too) and second on doxic and predicative consciousness. Using the example given before, on the first level my eyes are on my partner. On the second level, I want to do what my eyes are already doing. Thus, I reflect on what I am already doing and decide to willingly do what my eyes are already doing.

This means that the foundational ground of volitions is axiological on a lower level and doxic on a higher one. It is axiological because I ponder the affections that awaken me[3]; it is doxic because I acknowledge the feelings that I decide to determine in a doxic thesis. I want something first because I value my goal and second because I believe in its correctness. The grounding theses are the primitive compass for any kind of act (Hua XXVIII, 142). The belief in what is about to happen comes from an act of willing (Hua XXVIII, 122). "All reason is at the same time practical reason" Husserl writes (1973, 308), "all acts (…) are modes of willing, modes of behavior rooted in a capacity of the I (…) Judging is a way of willing in a widest sense" (A V, 22, 5). The representation of what we want to pursue arises from a background of beliefs related to real being (Hua XXVIII, 122). My operating will can predicate the affections of my not-operating will; indeed the latter moves the former to the act of predication and the former allows the latter to be recognizable. Theoretical and practical reasons are at once reason; judging and willing cannot be conceived as separated from each other. Willing and correlatively the position of willing (its intention) are based upon and regulated by the primordial bodily evidence that affects the will and turns its thesis into values and representations. Every operating willing act presupposes a general representation of what a given volition wants on the basis of a wide background of beliefs and values related to hyletic being (Hua XXVIII, 122–24). The goal of operating willing lies in what we recognize as objectively given. According to Husserl, I simply pose something and I pose this something as a practical and predicative ought (*Sollen*) (Hua XXVIII, 128). The highest goal lies in the operating will that aims at the best outcome among all that we can achieve in a given context (Hua XXVIII, 166).

Willing, Desiring and Time

For Husserl, willing is strictly connected to time. Husserl asserts (in Hua-Mat IX, 133 or Hua XXVIII, 103–112) that willing aims at practical realization, otherwise my volition would not be a volition but simply a desire. The basic characteristic of any volition is its possibility to be achieved ("*Erreichenbarkeit*").

While willing something is the practical *analogon* of certitude (doxic position in Husserl's vocabulary) and it can be modified according to hypotheses or disjunctive modifications of willing (Hua XXVIII, 127), desire is the practical analogon of the question (here we mean "question" in the Latin sense of the word as *quaero*; that is, asking a question without any expectation to receive an answer in return). Willing, which for Husserl is parallel to the certitude of belief, poses its thesis in the future as a certainty. I want something means that my willing is certain to be able to reach its wanted object in the future (Hua XXVIII, 121–122). The difference between wanting and desiring another person's body lies upon the strength of achievability of my goal in the future. The future becomes a field of concrete achievement of my volition. Volitions' goals can be fulfilled and find their concretization only in the future; before volitions are achieved they exist only as ideals (Hua XXVIII, 123). In that sense volitions are creative acts, while desires (as we will see in the next section) are tendencies that arise in the present and tend toward the future without posing the future as certain. If I desire someone, it is because maybe a part of me knows that I cannot have that person as much as I want; while if I want someone I am convinced that I am going to attain what I am looking for. Following this interpretation it seems that the difference between the two is just a matter of confidence in what one pursues. What cannot be easily attained is expressible only in the form of a desire.

Differently from joy or desire, volitions are always directed to what is real, the sphere of ideal is completely precluded from it as is the sphere of the past (Hua XXVIII, 123). I cannot reasonably want what has been achieved in the past, because I know that my sense of time is not reversible. Yet I can feel sexual desires toward the past because I do not necessarily strive for its achievements. Volitions' theses do not refer only to the now and to its creator, but also to the subsequent temporal extension and its contents. Willing is expressed in the present through its creative *fiat*, but tends toward the future as a creator that constitutes its goal as reality in the action (Hua XXVIII, 125). A creative realization can take place only when reality appears or when we are not yet aware of its presence, because as any creation it takes its origin from nothing (Hua XXVIII, 126). Consequently, the two steps that separate the not-operating from the operating will has to do with time and its phenomenological structure of retentions and protentions.

Volitions need reality and reality needs future in order to become. According to Husserl, willings are acts that belong to the emotional sphere (*Gemüt*) and they are different from other kinds of acts because they refer only to what is going to be real in the future (Hua XXVIII, 122). Willing begins in a now, but always refers to the chain of protentions and retentions in which the act comes to existence. Any volition is directed to the future because its acts always refer to what the willing has not yet created (Hua X, section 26). The thesis of willing does not relate only to the now and its creative beginning, but also to the future that makes the willing an operative and positive one (Hua XXVIII, 125).

It is important to remark that the bridge from not-operating to operating will—that is, thesis in the now and its *fiat*—is characterized by egolessness and ego awakening. When the sexual instinct comes to pose its thesis as a will in the now, it is not an egoic will that is posed, but a passive whole of hyletic syntheses that strive toward a protensive direction[4] (Hua XV, 594). In the transition from instincts to not-operating and finally operating will the ego is the very last layer to appear. The lower level of will-intentionality is moved by an egoless force which aims at a loosely oriented determination; while the higher level of will-intentionality has an ego-pole from which the actual will can be reconstructed and recollected. We know that we want something only through the recollection of what has been retained in the past. Although actual will cannot be in the past, its chance to be visible for us passes only through the recollection of its past and its retention which can happen only if there is an ego accompanying this recollection.[5]

In the next section I will explain what I mean by intentionality and to what kind of intentionality I am referring in these pages.

Husserl's Theory of Intentionalities

On a sexual level the two layers—egoless and egoic, not-operating and operating will—fluidly intertwine because of their peculiar form of intentionality, namely the intentionality of instincts and more specifically what Husserl called intentionality of copulation[6] (Hua XV, 596).

The intentionality of copulation represents for Husserl a form of fulfillment (Hua XV, 596) of the intentionality of instincts. As I clarified in the previous chapter the intentionality of instincts cannot be considered as the same kind of intentionality that Husserl describes in *Logical Investigations*. As Bower (2014) remarked, intentionality of instincts and intentionality of affections belong to the same kind of passive and egoless intentionality that aims at enjoyment and fulfillment.

Given the wide number of intentionalities used by Husserl, I distinguished at least three categories of intentionalities: active, passive, and practical. While active intentionality entails a position-taking (*Stellungnahme*) and a meaning-giving (*Sinngebung*) activity (Hua III), passive intentionality is a synthetic process that takes place mainly on two egoless layers, spontaneous and non-spontaneous syntheses (Hua XXXIII). These layers constitute the material core around which the meaning-giving activity of the active intention revolves. The transition from the egoless synthetic process to the egoic meaning-giving (*Sinngebung*) activity is marked out by the practical intention. In fact, the sphere of irritability (Hua XXXIII, text 1)—that is, the layer of affections and reactions— represents the lowest level of affections from which the ego emerges and reacts to the irritating affecting matter by deciding what position it is going to take (Hua XXXIII, text 1, 5, 6, 9, 10). The reactive emergence stems from the volitional body (Hua-Mat IV, 186) which bridges together nature (passive syntheses) and spirit (active intention); the ego reacts to the matter by deciding whether to accept and validate that matter as its own. Some of the material content provided to the ego will remain in the form of passive syntheses, other material will be organized through values and meanings. While the realm of passivity provides the formless matter with a logical or graspable form, the realm of activity is the constitutive pole through which a given number of synthetic layers are comprised in a graspable meaning. The practical intention is that phrenetic act through which the subject decides to move toward a self-constituting act in recognizing the interconnection between passive syntheses and its own activity. The bridge between active intention and passive synthesis is represented by the practical intention, the "Ich will und Ich tue" which operates through the means of the volitional body in order to awake (Hua-Mat IX, 128–129, 133) the ego to its present matter.

Instinct Intentionality and Intentionality of Copulation

Husserl describes the instinctive force of the intentionality of copulation as the one which moves matter toward procreation and the constitution of a Mitwelt.[7] Hence, even the "not-operating" sex, which is not properly moved by a generative goal, holds the inner agenda of creating a shared community of monads. Affectant and affected matter fuse together in a correlation directed to the Other. To paraphrase Husserl, primordiality is a system of instincts that we understand as a permanent passive flow which intersects the flow of other subjects (*Ichsubjekten*). The intentionality that moves this primordiality holds the transcendental goal of reaching out for foreign others (Hua XV, 594).[8] Its passive primordial flow intersects other flows and awakes the ego subject within the practical intention; that is, within the awareness of being in that moment. It is through the awakening of the practical intention that the active intention can objectify the content of the passive flow and assign a meaning to that intersubjective intersection.

Hence, the primordiality of the passive flow is regulated by a universal teleology that leads to a universal form of egoless intentionality whose wholeness lies in a system of fulfillments. As Husserl remarks, this form of universal intentionality is an ongoing primordial constitution, a living present whose I is de-centered. The absolute simultaneity of all the monads establishes a dialogue through the universal system of instincts which transcends the actual limit of my ego flow or my understanding of it. It is from this interplay that the ego awakes to its own life and discovers itself as the center of acts in reference to a surrounding world. This new awakening creates every time a new world horizon in the community of human beings[9] (Hua XV, 595–596).

Through the fulfillment of the intentionality of copulation the new I might awake in a new ontological structure that defines its specific character, a relationship, a cathartic scene, an intimate connection. The world of instincts, the world of organisms is a generative and organic unity whose actual goal is the spiritual and bodily procreation of new organisms (Hua XV, 601–602).[10] The passage from egoless to egoic layers is always procreative whether it brings forth an actual new life or new awareness within a Mitwelt.

The community of love that Husserl describes refers precisely on its lower and most egoless level to this generative community of instincts in which our operating and not-operating will are aimed at the fulfillment of doxic and axiological goals[11]; i.e., goals that can be recollected and explained through a meaning thanks to the objectivating character of active intentionality or goals whose quality is merely affective and can be felt through the awakenings of the practical intention.

Sexual Habits

> The personal Ego constitutes itself not only as a person determined by *drives* (…) but *also as a higher, autonomous, freely acting* Ego, in particular one guided by *rational motives*…. Habits are necessarily formed, just as much with regard to originally instinctive behavior (…) as with regard to free behavior. To yield to a drive establishes the drive to yield: habitually. Likewise, to let oneself be determined by a value-motive and to resist a drive establishes a tendency (a "drive") to let oneself be determined once again by such a value-motive (…) and to resist these drives.
>
> *(Hua IV, 255; En. tr. 267)*

Husserl describes here the circle that generates the personal Ego. In fact, instincts and habits are two poles that shape our personal identity. On the one hand, instincts arise as original instincts and affections; on the other, habits are inhibitions and reinforcements of the primal instincts. According to Husserl, our personality, and accordingly our sexual character, takes shape through this cycle. Our personality is built upon habits, while affections and instincts break through the solid structure of personality changing its core.

As Husserl puts it in his researches on *intersubjectivity*:

> I am not only an actual but I am also a habitual ego, and habituality signifies a certain egoic possibility, an "I can" or "I could", or "I would have been able to", and this ability become actual refers to ego–actualities, to actual ego–experiences, that is, as actualization of

ability. In a word, I am (and without this would not be an I, I can not think of myself otherwise), an ego of capacities.

(Hua XIV, 378)

"I am an *actual* but I am also a *habitual* ego." I am what I happen to be in the present through my primal affections and instincts which sexually manifest in the form of impulses and desires; but I am also all the possibilities and actualities that I decide to reiterate in the future. I am my core of instincts and habits. My personal character is my impersonal present, which keeps on arising in a chain of impersonal nows[12] on which in fact I build my personality. My character endures as a synthesis of my ongoing affirmations of affections and instincts, stretching toward the future from an arising present. This does not mean that I consciously choose who I am, because it is impossible to be fully aware of all my passive life of impulses, drives and desires; but by reiterating some of them as habits I can choose a part of me in which I want to endure. In the *Cartesian Meditations* section 32, Husserl describes *habitus* as a lasting "state" (*dauerender Habitus*) that I decide in a wakeful choice to keep in present and reiterate in my future. It is this endurance that constitutes my stable and abiding ego with its "personal character" (Hua I, 67; En. tr. 101). As Lee remarks, instincts are Uraffektionen (1993, 166), in the sense that they are what originally awakens us and calls us to be. They are what is there for the ego (Hua-Mat VIII, 351). "Original affection is an instinct, thus a kind of empty striving still lacking the presentation of a goal" (Hua-Mat VIII, 253). In that sense, the myth of Psyche and Cupido as it is told in Ovid's Metamorphoses teaches us that when we find love, erotic love, we find our psyche too. Paying attention to our Uraffektionen is a way for the ego to awake and discover its inner organic character.

"A desiderative life—*Desiring life*—positively directs itself (...) toward pure enjoying. Conversely a non-desiderative—*Desiring negatively*—directs itself against all breaking in of what is negatively pleasant (Negativ-Lustigem) against all decreases, disruptions" (Hua-Mat VIII, 340). Instincts, similarly to desires, are guided by pleasure (Hua-Mat VIII, 331) and call for acceptances or negations. The more volitive I am in a given moment, the more I reinforce the structure of my habitual personality and the less space would be given to the arising egoless desiderative life. This is so in the sense that willfully reaffirming my habits simultaneously reaffirms my personal character, with the result, in Husserl's words, of feeling "pleasure in recognizing what is the same"

(Hua-Mat VIII, 331), a pleasure that cannot be assimilated to the sensuous egoless one.

Both desires, which draw the arc of instincts-affections arising in the present, and volitions, which express themselves in the arc of habits and reality in the future, are important components of the sexual life.

Conclusion

This chapter described how sexual life arises as an egoless hyletic life that is put in motion by passive intentionality, coitus intentionality, and is transformed into active intentionality, namely a meaning-giving activity. This analysis confirms how while sex represents a basic need of our intersubjective and generative life, it is enjoyable even when disconnected from this basic need because it keeps the individual in contact with the lowest organic matter of its life.

According to Husserl, on its lower level sexual life is moved by instincts, drives, impulses and aims at the fulfillment of desiderative life that ultimately seems to be directed at the procreation. On its higher level sexual life is moved by the not-operating and operating will which allows the transition from an hyletic egoless flow to the awakening of the ego as intersecting other flows. On this level the ultimate goal of the sexual life is the constitution of a Mitwelt—which we might call family, state, relationship—in which the ego wakes up and builds its own life. Both levels contribute in different ways to the constitution of the sexual personality; the cycle of active acceptance or negation of some of the ongoing flow of lower instincts, drives, and impulses is what guides the formation of a habitual character. Sensuous pleasure can arise on both layers, either as fulfillment of the immediate goal of the instincts or as a fulfillment of the habitual tendency to recognize the same.

Notes

1 Cf. on this point Melle, U. "Husserls Phänomenologie des Willens," Tijdschrift voor Filosopfie 54/2 (1992), 280–305; Mertens, K. (1998) "Husserl's Phenomenology of the Will in his Reflections on Ethics," in *Alterity and Facticity: New Perspectives on Husserl*, (eds. Depraz, N. and Zahavi, D.), Dordrecht, Kluwer Academic Publishers.

2 Cf. also Husserl, (1973) section 48.

3 As I proved elsewhere (Bloomsbury, 2015) Husserl is influenced by Lozte's way of intending axiology as that form of rationality that validates being as such and infers data through *ratio* and *proportio*. As Husserl wrote, in that sense

"The moral sentiment (*Gemüt*) and the will are a proper sources of legitimacy and authenticity" (Hua XLII, 241).

4 Hua XV, 594: "In meiner alten Lehre vom inneren Zeitbewusstsein habe ich die hierbei aufgewiesene Intentionalität eben als Intentionalität, als Protention vorgerichtet und als Retention sich modifizierend, aber Einheit bewahrend, behandelt, aber nicht vom Ich gesprochen, nicht sie als ichliche (im weitesten Sinn Willensintentionalität) charakterisiert. Später habe ich die letztere als in einer ichlosen ("Passivität") fundierte eingeführt."

5 Hua XV, 595: "Später habe ich die letztere als in einer ichlosen ("Passivität") fundierte eingeführt. Die Rückfrage und Rekonstruktion führt auf die ständige Zentrierung durch den Ichpol jeder Primordialität, der ständig Pol bleibt in ständigem Gang der Objektivation, in der auf der weltlichen Seite das objektivierte Ich mit seinem Leib steht."

6 Hua XV, 596:

> Ich gehe von mir Menschen aus und auf meine menschliche Monade, darin direkt impliziert meine menschliche Mitwelt. Frage nach der Intentionalität der Kopulation. In der Trieberfüllung liegt, unmittelbar gesehen, nichts von dem erzeugten Kind, nichts davon, dass es im anderen Subjekt die bekannten Folgen hat und schliesslich die Mutter das Kind gebärt.

7 Hua XV, 593, 4:

> Das Interne der Zeugung. Trieb zum anderen Geschlecht. Der Trieb in dem einen Individuum und der Wechseltrieb im anderen. Der Trieb kann im Stadium des unbestimmten Hungers sein, das seinen Gegenstand noch nicht als sein Worauf in sich trägt. (...) Im Fall des Geschlechtshungers in bestimmter Richtung auf sein affizierendes, reizendes Ziel ist dieses der Andere. Dieser bestimmte Geschlechtshunger hat Erfüllungsgestalt im Modus der Kopulation. (...) 593 Im Trieb selbst liegt die Bezogenheit auf den Anderen als Anderen und auf seinen korrelativen Trieb. Der eine und andere Trieb kann den Modus—Abwandlungsmodus—der Enthaltung, des Widerwillens haben. Im Urmodus ist er eben "hemmungslos" unmodalisierter Trieb, der je in den Anderen hineinreicht und seine Triebintentionalität durch die korrelative im Anderen hindurchreichen hat.

8 Husserl, E III, 5:

> Ich denke hier an die Probleme Eltern, oder vor allem, Mutter und Kind, die aber auch im Zusammenhang der Kopulationsproblematik erwachsen. Die Primordialität ist ein Triebsystem. Wenn wir sie verstehen als urtümlich stehendes Strömen, so liegt darin auch jeder in andere Ströme, und mit evtl. anderen Ichsubjekten, hineinstrebende Trieb. Diese Intentionalität hat ihr transzendentes "Ziel", transzendent

als eingeführtes Fremdes, und doch in der Primordialität als eigenes Ziel, also ständig ihren Kern urmodaler, sich schlicht erhebender und erfüllender Intention.

9 Hua XV, 595, 6:

> Das würde zur Auffassung einer universalen Teleologie führen, als einer universalen Intentionalität als sich einstimmig in der Einheit eines totalen Erfüllungssystems erfüllenden. Die Frage ist dann, wie die Ichzentrierung zu verstehen ist in der Universalität der intentionalen Implikation in der standing konstituierten all-primordialen urtümlichen lebendigen Gegenwart, der absoluten "Simultaneität" aller Monaden, durch wechselseitiges unmittelbares und mittelbares Transzendieren von Trieben vergemeinschafteten Monaden. Das neue Erwachen von lehen als eigentlichen, als Zentren von Akten in bezug auf eine Umwelt, also Erwachen von Konstitutionen von "Seienden", schliesslich eines Welthorizontes – als in der universalen Teleologie mitbeschlossene Teleologie, als der immerfort sich "steigernden" totalen Intentionalität in der fortwachsenden Lebendigkeit einer einheitlichen bewusstseinsmässigen Monadengemeinschaft. Diese ist universal konstituierte Triebgemeinschaft, ihr entspricht im Strömen jeweils horizonthaft schon seiende Welt, wonach sie in sich immer wieder Monaden zur gesteigerten Ausbildung, zur "Entwicklung" bringt und immer schon gebracht hat. In dieser Form kommt die Totali tät der Monaden in Abschlagszahlungen zum Selbstbewusstsein, zuhöchst universal als Menschengemeinschaft.

10 Hua XV, 601–602:

> Wir wachsen in der Familie und durch sie in völkischer Gemeinschaft. Wir wachsen in sie hinein, wir wachsen stufenweise in ihre Umwelt hinein, und so in der Tierwelt. Unser Verständnis erweitert sich, unsere Welterfahrung, unsere Weltapperzeption baut sich aus. Sind wir reif geworden, so ist die reife Welt selbst nur einigermassen fest in ihrer allgemeinen ontologischen Struktur und in einer besonderen traditionalen Typik. Wir können nun Welterkenntnis zum Thema machen, Historie, Naturhistorie. Menschliche generative Zusammenhänge, unsere historische Welt. Die Tierwelt, die Welt der Organismen, die Einheit der organischen Generation – in ihr als ein Zweig die menschliche Generation.

11 Husserl, cit. in Yamaguchi, I, (1992) *Passive Synthesis und Intersubjektivitaet by Husserl*, Den Hagues: Martinus Nijhoff, 131:

> Will ich als Liebender mit, in meinen universalen Lebenswillen habe ich den des Anderen aufgenommen, in dem aktuellen Zusammensein mit ihm verstehe ich nicht nur den Gang der Verwirklichung seines personalen und letztpersonalen Strebens nach, dieses damit zugleich näher kennenlernend, sondern ich eigne es mir ständig an und bin

schon in der Willensrichtung von da an, wo ich Freundschaft mit ihm begründet habe (wo die Urstiftung der Liebe—in ihren verschiedenen Formen—eingesetzt hat). Persönlichkeit bezogen auf die Totalität des Willenslebens—so auf die Totalität des Ich in seinem Sein. In der Liebe einseitige oder in der Wechselliebe wechselseitige "Deckung", Verschmelzung der Personen, deren jede doch von "ihrer Stelle aus" ihr Leben hat, ihr aktuelles erfahrendes, denkendes, handelndes Leben, ihre eigenen Akterwerbe, ihre Habitualitäten, ihre Interessen. Aber hier die Probleme der konkreten Ermöglichung der personalen Liebeseinigung als dauernder, wie es ständig in ihrem Sinn ist. Zweieinigkeit der Personen, Einheit des sich vergemeinschaftenden totalen Lebens und Strebens.

12 In Merleau-Ponty's language "anonymous" now (see Levin, D. "Eros and Psyche" in *Pathways into the Jungian World*).

Bibliography

Bower, M. (2014). "Intentionality of Instincts as a Theory of Affection." *Journal of the British Society for Phenomenology*, vol. 45, no. 2, 133–147.

Dickinson, E. R. (2002). "Sex, Masculinity, and the 'Yellow Peril': Christian Von Ehrenfels' Program for a Revision of the European Sexual Order, 1902–1910." *German Studies Review*, vol. 25, no. 2, 255–284.

Husserl, E. (1973a). *Zur Phänomenologie der Intersubjektivität. Texte aus dem Nachlass. Zweiter Teil. 1921–28*, (ed. Kern, I.). The Hague: Martinus Nijhoff.

Husserl, E. (1973b). *Zur Phänomenologie der Intersubjektivität. Texte aus dem Nachlass. Dritter Teil. 1929–35*, (ed. Kern, I.). The Hague: Martinus Nijhoff.

Husserl, E. (1988). *Vorlesungen über Ethik und Wertlehre, 1908–1914*, (ed. Melle, U.). The Hague: Kluwer Academic Publishers.

Husserl, E. (2001). *Die Bernauer 'Manuskripte' über das Zeitbewußtsein (1917/18)*, (ed. Bernet, R. and Lohmar, D.). Dordrecht: Kluwer Academic Publishers.

Husserl, E. (2002). *Natur und Geist. Vorlesungen Sommersemester 1919*, (ed. Weiler, M.). Dordrecht: Kluwer Academic Publishers.

Husserl, E. (2004). *Einleitung in die Ethik 1920/1924*, (ed. Peucker, H.). Dordrecht/Boston/London: Kluwer Academic Publishers.

Husserl, E. (2006). *Späte Texte über Zeitkonstitution (1929–1934). Die C-Manuskripte*, (ed. Lohmar, D.). New York: Springer.

Husserl, E. (2012). *Einleitung in die Philosophie. Vorlesungen 1916–1919*, (ed. Jacobs, H.). Dordrecht: Springer.

Lee, N. (1999). "La phénomélogie des tonalites affectives chez Edmund Husserl," *Alter*, vol. 7, 243–250.

Melle, U. (1992). "Husserls Phänomenologie des Willens," *Tijdschrift voor Filosofie 54*(2) 280–305.

Mertens, K. (1998). "Husserl's Phenomenology of the Will in his Reflections on Ethics," in *Alterity and Facticity: New Perspectives on Husserl*, 121–138, (ed. Depraz, N. and Zahavi, D.). Dordrecht: Kluwer Academic Publishers.

3

PERVERSIONS

Introduction

While in the previous chapter *eros* was examined as a powerful drive that can bring the individual closer to one's inner self, in this chapter I will describe how this same erotic force can lead to a split between one's intimate personality and the social persona. In particular, I will conduct a phenomenological analysis of paraphilia by applying Husserl's theory of practical intentionality on a case of masochism cited in the DSM-IV.

Hence, the chapter will be divided into two sections. The first will be dedicated to a philosophical discussion of Nagel, Sartre and Cowan's writings about sadism and masochism. In the second part I will discuss the ground prepared by these authors to continue a phenomenological discussion of masochism and its hyletic roots.

It is my belief that paraphilia, both in its masochistic and sadistic declension, might represent a way to come in contact with the egoless organic layer of Being I referred to in the previous chapter. Paraphilic drives, if lived with awareness, have the power to challenge one's individual volitional body and to invite to a moral exploration that, when pursued, would restitute meanings to one's lived-experiences. Since these drives might not meet social expectations, it is rare for an individual to achieve reflective awareness in relation to these erotic layers; the blame carried out by the moral intersubjective stigma often suffocates any attempt to awareness, thus generating imbalanced responses. Hence, this chapter will focus on the split that might be generated in one's intimate life in response to a paraphilic sexual preference. Although Husserl's notion of intersubjective validation can offer a key to interpret paraphilia from a political and social point of view, I will limit my analysis only to the intrapsychic individual's life and I will defer the other levels of description to my final chapters' discussion of *agape*, social, and political love.

What is a Perversion?

According to its etymology, perversion refers to a disruptive attitude exercised toward ourselves or others; in Latin *per-versus* points to someone who subverts a natural harmonic order in order to pursue a deceptive and corrupting aim.

Since 1876 the masochistic and sadistic quality of erotic compulsions have been categorized as a paraphilic disorder, a pathology that promoted immorality. The current edition of the DSM categorizes as paraphilic those behaviors that have been criminalized as leading and accordingly considered to disruptive within the society; from a legal point of view a person is affected from this disorder when she can be recognized as a sexual offender and there is a case for her to be legally sentenced.[1] According to Krueger (2006), to whose literature review I defer since I do not have space to discuss it here, sexual masochism and sadism are a form of paraphilic coercive disorders that is considered as separated from other forms of paraphilia. In particular, according to DSM-IV, sexual masochism disorder (SMD) is the condition of experiencing recurring and intense sexual arousal in response to enduring moderate or extreme pain, suffering, or humiliation, while sexual sadism refers to causing pain, humiliation, fear, or some form of physical or mental harm to another person in order to achieve sexual gratification. In both cases, the negative quality of the word *perversion* seems to pervade this phenomenon both from a conceptual and clinical point of view. As I will show in the next section Nagel and Sartre give a philosophical account for the reason why paraphilic attitudes should be considered as a deviation of erotic drives, while Cowan will show how by taking at least a neutral position in relation to this phenomenon one would be capable of more deeply understanding the layers of erotic necessity embodied in these phenomena. Personally, I think that a position of neutrality would invite a wider moral exploration of the intimate life, whether one's own or that of others, which would allow a deeper contact with the self whose experience is labelled as paraphilic.

Nagel's Reading

Nagel (1997) builds his theory upon Sartre's although with some variations and distance. According to Nagel, perversion cannot be associated with all that is considered socially unnatural, otherwise we should call "perverted" all the sexual activity that does not aim at reproduction. Nagel considers perversions a psychological phenomenon that does not elicit a healthy sexual encounter for two main reasons.

First, perversion is a psychological phenomenon rather than a physiological one because if sexual desires were equated to physiological phenomena like hunger, then anything could be sexual and anything could be considered perverted. Hence perversion, as much as any sexual phenomenon, finds its roots in our psyche rather than in our body.

Second, drawing on Sartre's theory, Nagel proposes that in a healthy sexual encounter each person becomes aware of him/herself by a mutual recognition between partners. From this psychological recognition of their mutual existence stems a sense of well-being that induces the partners to stay with each other and look after each other.

According to Nagel's reading, in a paraphilic encounter the recognition is perverted because the partners remain stuck on the level of the flesh. Using the word *perversion* in agreement with the negative sense that its etymology seems to evoke, Nagel considers perversion a psychological truncation (1969, 15, 16). The person who experiences a perverted sexual encounter seems to remain stuck at the level of the flesh without coming to existence through an actual encounter with his/her partner. "The truncated or incomplete versions of the complete configuration (…) may therefore be regarded as perversions of the central impulse" (1969, 14). When the desire of the partners does not bring to a mutual recognition, the encounter is deprived of the mutual recognition of arousal; in this case, the "perverted" person remains subject or object of the sexual experience without drawing the psychological and physical pleasure that "normally" should derive from a fulfilling sexual experience.

Sartre

If Nagel's analysis of perversion implies a pessimistic view about the possibility of people who enjoy perversion to live a psychologically fulfilling life, Sartre's judgment is even stronger. In Chapter 3 of Part III of *Being and Nothingness* Sartre uses the word *failure* four times in relation to sexual perversions (1956, 378–389); perversions, he states, are "a failure of love" (1957, 378–388).

For Sartre love is what "makes me be" (366). Similarly to what Nagel recognized, an erotic encounter is not just a means to physical possessions, otherwise love would be very easily satisfied (1957, 376), but it is the way through which my facticity is recognized and becomes truly existent (1957, 377). From this point of view love—which is not distinct here from agapic or erotic love—reveals the freedom of one's transcendence (1957, 374). "Love as the primitive relation to the other is the ensemble of the projects by which I am good at realizing this value" (1957, 366).

Through Love Desire is Fulfilled

The question is: what is desire? Desire for what? Why do we desire? To answer these questions Sartre cites Husserl's notion of affective intentionality. When we desire, we dispose our being in a particular mode that is neither exclusively physical nor exclusively mental. There is a tension that needs to be fulfilled. Affective intentionality does not refer to a positional consciousness[2] (1957, 386), rather it is a tension toward something that can be fulfilled in different ways. Hence, according to Sartre, I am moved to desire someone because of the engulfment of the world in my flesh and what I desire is "to be overcome" (1957, 385). I am moved by desire because my body is organically alive and through my desire I want to be overwhelmed and I want to discover the absolute that brought my and partner's facticity into being as being chosen by the absolute of God (1957, 377). Hence, according to Sartre, desire is a meaning that is assigned to human condition (1957, 383–384).

Consequently, standing by this definition of desire and love, sadism and masochism are a failure of love because they induce one to a behavior that does not allow any actual liberation or recognition of oneself. In love I am possessed by the other and I can exist in and with the other's witnessing of my factual being (1957, 361, 365), while in sadistic love this possession is treated as a form of property that does not lead to any recognition (1957, 402). According to Sartre, the way in which sadists handle freedom leads to an ambiguous situation; the sadist in fact tries to appropriate the freedom of the partner although it might happen that the partner can decide when to stop the scene. According to Sartre, both in sadism and masochism, the incarnation of the Other takes place through violence, appropriation, and use of the Other (1957, 399). Therefore love fails its purpose because the desire of being overwhelmed is achieved only in a fake way and is not acted in absolute spontaneity and freedom. Lacking of this freedom, according to Sartre, a masochist cannot ever fully experience the abandonment to the "vertigo before falling in the abyss of other's objectivity," because both partners remain somehow vigilant and in charge of each other in an ambiguous way (1957, 378); they remain stuck in their subjectivity.

The Erotic Necessity

Cowan's position toward paraphilia is less negative than Sartre's and Nagel's positions. Citing Simone Weil she writes that "all love is sadistic because of the possessing feeling" that it evokes (1982, 76); when one loves, they want to possess the other person and their desire grows until this possession is not completed. It is as if erotic desire demands a submission to *Ananke* (the Necessity) as the lovers feel possessed by a power stronger than their own nature that compulsively pushes them toward unpredictable directions. What happens to us and our beloved ones when we fall for someone is not in our control, yet we surrender ourselves to our destiny (another way in which Greek translates the word *Ananke*) (1982, 41). Necessity is the Goddess that reveals Eros' presence. In book 5 of Republic Plato defines erotic desire as an irrational and disruptive force (458c8–d7) that involves shame and submission (61) in order that one gains contact with a deeper meaning that is held within the suffering (77, 101). As Barney (2008) remarks, Plato

> brings out the more particular point that eros as a cause of epistemic ascent could be understood as a kind of compulsion. (...) To desire erotically is to seek immortality through creative union with something perceived as beautiful: and that is an inherently insatiable desire for what is by nature most powerfully attractive to us.
>
> *(28)*

Hence eros is revealed to us by a masochistic and sadistic necessity to act against our own nature in order to ascent to a deeper meaning that puts us in contact with real beauty and harmony. According to Cowan, erotic desire frustrates ego's intentions (1982, 51, 49, 65), yet by doing so it leads to a path of true individuation and pleasure.[3]

Phenomenological Account of Perversions

In this second part I will use Husserl's theory of practical intentionality with a twofold goal: first, to describe paraphilic drives in order to understand the meanings that can be possibly attached to these drives; second, to understand what quality of love can be recognized in connection with them.

Phenomenology of Mind-Body

While Nagel's interpretation seems to introduce a distinction between the physiological and the psychological layer of the phenomenon of paraphilia, Husserl's phenomenology considers body and mind as a whole (Ferrarello, 2015). In phenomenology the mind-body unit points to a steady process of mutual recognition and integration that unfolds itself through intentionality.[4]

This process of unfolding starts with motility and the act of ownership that follows movement, for example "my hand is moving" or "I can move my hand." Although it seems to be a small achievement, the mind-body connection lies mainly in that realization. Through the "I can" "I become the initiating point of a host of causalities" (Husserl, 1983). My body becomes for me a kinaesthetic system that indicates the interlacing of the perception of those movements that allow me to feel tacitly aware of myself as occupying space. Similarly, Merleau-Ponty writes that one's body is a kinaesthetic system reduced into a representation because of the inadequacy of my perception (1962, 94). Motility is the basic intention that leads me to create bodily images as a compendium of all my bodily experiences (1962, 98). The nervous system receives stimuli that excite the body so that it reorganizes[5] those stimuli by transversal functioning (1962, 83).

In Hua-Mat IV, 10, Husserl describes the subject of a body as "a relativity of nature to spirit"; the subject is what questions the status quo of its being. When the I arises from its undifferentiated matter and questions the meaning of what its matter is, then the subject is born, and this subject will remain a subject for an undefined period of time.

Consequently, for Husserl the body is an aesthesiological unit (Hua-Mat IV, 281), an original field of possibilities (*Urfeld of koennens*) in which its undifferentiated matter that is not yet owned by a subject becomes a living thing and then a living body bearer of sensations (Hua IV, 183). It is on this level that different sorts of erotic drives start pushing on the subject demanding it to take their ownership. Taking ownership does not imply their fulfillment, but just the acknowledgment of their existence as related to that body.

The way in which the subject perceives the body and comes to own it as its own is described by Husserl through layers. Differently from what Carman noticed (1999) these layers are not cognitive, but rather functional in that they describe the corporeal function of the subject relating to them. The thing becomes an organic body (*Koerper*) because it can move, and it is through this movement that a witness within the body realizes that it can perceive itself in space and time. This witness comes through an "Ich will" (I want) that mediates between the "Ich kann" (I can) and the "Ich tue" (I act). The "I want," as we will see in the next section, represents an important layer that Husserl calls "volitional body" which, as "connecting bridge between nature and spirit" (Hua-Mat IV, 186) has the goal of mediating between bodily and spiritual decisions, thus allowing individual's functionings. This layer as standing in between material and spiritual layers (*Ich tue* and *Ich kann*) facilitates the process of becoming a subject within a body.

These three layers—organic, volitional, and living body—are characterized by a different form of intention: passive, practical, and active intention, that I am going to describe in more detail in the next section.

Passive, Active, and Practical Intentionality

In Chapter 2 I gave an extensive account of practical intentionality, here I will return to the analysis of the relationship between practical, active, and passive intentionality in order to provide an interpretive grid to analyze the phenomenon of paraphilia. In *Analyses Concerning Passive and Active Syntheses* (2001) Husserl describes passive intentionality as an egoless form of intention that is expressed through a complex combination of spontaneous and non-spontaneous syntheses. The first layer of spontaneous synthesis, that of *Sinnlichkeit*, is the layer in which being and being perceived are assembled together through a constant rhythm of pulsation (2001, 204) that takes place without the ego. The synthesis happens because the affectant and the affected are fused together (*Logical Investigations*, 2001, VI, 47) and come to association according to a principle of homogeneity that assigns a sensuous meaning to the association. On the second associative layer, which is not spontaneous because it involves the predicative effort of an ego that is not fully there yet, the homogenous sensuous cluster becomes a thematic object of an ego. Yet, before the ego becomes fully active there is a process of validation first in which he accepts or refuses the hyletic syntheses. In the case of erotic drives, on a spontaneous layer one's body might call for sexual pleasure, which means that the blood pressure would rise and the hormonal balance would change. On the level of non-spontaneous synthesis one might decide to own these phenomena and accept their sensuous meaning by acting upon them. The interconnection of non-spontaneous and spontaneous syntheses produces in an individual an awakening that its ego might recognize, accept, and transform into units of understandable meanings. In the case of masochistic or sadistic drives it might happen that the non-spontaneous syntheses do not arrive at producing meanings because the sensuous matter operating at the spontaneous layer was not fully accepted.

The words *acceptance* and *refusal* need to be taken in a very broad sense. The first form of acceptance concerns the acceptance of the sensuous information as belonging to one's body and the second form of acceptance has to do with the meanings one wants to assign to that information. The acceptance and refusal passes through the volitional body who transforms the *Ich kann* into an *Ich tue* (I can, therefore I do). Imagine the case of a person with an artificial limb and the case of a person with a numb limb. The acceptance of sensuous input coming from these two different bodies on the part of the volitional body will arrive at a different speed and with a different level of certainty. Independent of the genuineness of our matter, becoming an active subject requires first of all the acceptance of one's being bound to that specific body and then the effort of making meanings coming out of that acceptance. In the case of paraphilic drives, the meaning-making act is often prevented from the volitional refusal of the first layer of spontaneous synthesis. In fact, after the acceptance or refusal, the volitional body has to decide whether to acknowledge the ownership upon the syntheses, and on a more refined level whether to act upon them or not—the action can be as simple as recognizing their moral or cognitive meaning. For example, I feel the need to go to the bathroom (first level). I can decide to go because I can move and get there (second level), yet I have to deny my body to take that action, because I realize that in this moment I am talking in front of a class (moral-cognitive level). This last third level, stemming from the intersection of the first and second level, is what in the second chapter I called "practical intentionality."

This form of intentionality stems from a here-now: a point in time and space from which the ego awakens and makes its decisions to be a subject bound to that body; to move in that body; to do the right thing through that body. These three layers all belong to the same source of validation stemming from the same point in time, the volitional body, a mind-body crossroads.

A Phenomenological Interpretation of Perversion

It is possible to notice how damaging is the disalignment between non-spontaneous and spontaneous syntheses in the case of sadistic drives.

DSM-IV reports the experience of a 25-year-old female student who was later diagnosed as a masochist. The woman required a consultation because she was depressed, and she had problems at work and with her husband. She started losing her emotional stability when two years earlier she discovered herself to be sexually aroused when her husband was screaming at her or was in a rage with her. Unconsciously, since then, she tried to find a way to provoke his rage. With the passing of time her behavior started undermining their relationship, and one year before her consultation their arguments ended up with her rushing out of the house and going to a bar for singles in order to pick up a man and get him to slap her. Slowly, she came to realize that she enjoyed receiving physical punishment.

Yet, when she came to her consultation, she did not mention the newly acquired awareness in relation to her sexual preference, but she presented herself as being depressed because of the state of her marriage—the meaning was there, but clearly it was not sufficiently deep. In her case the masochistic drives were acknowledged as an actual disorder because they became disruptive to her sense of well-being.

If we apply the intentional grid on this story, we can see how from a passive spontaneous level, a number of passive syntheses are prompting her to a factual reality that she is not eager to accept. Her arousal comes from being punished and hit. Yet, her volitional body does not allow the transition between spontaneous and non-spontaneous syntheses because she does not want to recognize herself as the owner of those feelings. This means that even if her ego awakens in front of the organic syntheses of her body, it is not allowed for her to assign them a meaning. This results in the complete loss of love, meant in this case as intimacy with erotic and organic drives. This misalignment prevents any body-mind connection to flow. Consequently, even if the body feels ready to achieve a certain form of sexual pleasure—and in fact, she seeks bars in search of satisfaction for her bodily pleasure or even provokes her husband to beat her—the active intention of her volitional body is completely dissociated. In this case the practical intentionality that awakes the volitional body does not trigger any alignment with the meaning-giving activity of the active intention. What results is the loss of a meaningful intimate space between herself and her body in which she could make caring and meaningful decisions for herself. She does not want to pay attention to the actual meaning that this new preference has in her life, therefore everything in her life starts collapsing: her emotional well-being, her intimate relationship with her husband, her effectiveness at work. Not being able to share herself with herself has a disruptive outcome in many areas of her life.

Hence, in her case it seems that the actual problem is not connected to her masochistic drives, but to a loss of intimacy with herself and her sexual preference. It seems that if she were able to understand her drives and accept the moral and cognitive challenge that they involve, she would have gathered a deeper quality of intimate love toward herself and her partner. If she were able to see what her body was asking from her and give it a meaning free from any preventive moral judgment her paraphilia would not have needed to be diagnosed. In this case, I believe that the actual problem was related to the fact that her body was not allowed to find any meaningful place where it could express itself in her daily and social life. Even if she decided not to act upon its paraphilic drives because she considered them dangerous for herself and her social community, I believe that it is still necessary to acknowledge them in a space that is free from moral judgments, otherwise any actual moral decision about them would be made without actual intimacy with one's inner self. In this case, the dialogue that takes place between her intentions is highly problematic and results in a conflict that does not leave space to any aware and meaningful shift. As a result she became a stranger to herself and to her husband, unable to function as she wished, at school or at home. Clearly, this is not due to the perversion itself but to the disalignment that its suppression entails. If she were able to connect with her organic needs, she would have gathered a deeper meaning about herself and her life.

This is to say that a paraphilic attitude does not necessarily entail the failure of love, as it does for Sartre, or the absence of mutual recognition as it does for Nagel. In this case the recognition of paraphilic drives would lead to a deeper loving bond with oneself that might have the taste of a compassionate intimacy.

Conclusion

In this chapter I discussed a case of paraphilia, masochism, using Husserl's theory of intentionality. I prepared the analysis using Sartre's and Nagel's phenomenological points of view, who condemn this lived-experience as a perversion of the natural need for mutual recognition. Using another philosophical point of view, such as Plato's, Weil's, and Cowan's,

I showed how a masochistic and sadistic quality might be intrinsic to the nature of love; and being able to explore this quality can foster the meaning that we can gather about our life.

By applying Husserl's theory to a case of paraphilia we were able to see how missing the opportunity to give meaning to a masochistic drive can lead to compulsive behaviors and prevent a person from understanding oneself in a meaningful way. Hence, love, meant also as masochism and sadism, can be a necessary force that pushes us toward a deeper understanding of ourselves. If we try to tame it, we would miss the opportunity to know who we really are.

Notes

1 First, M. B., "DSM-5 and Paraphilic Disorders," *American Academy Psychiatry Law*, vol. 42, no. 2, 191–201 (June 2014).
2 By *positional* here Husserl refers to an active act of consciousness in which the ego decides to take a position in relation to a specific phenomenon. I will talk more extensively about this in the last sections dedicated to the notion of the volitional body.
3 Even more strongly, in Moore's book on the analysis of De Sade's work and life, the author considers this form of "dark eros" as a viable opportunity for moral exploration (1998, 12, 105, 108). Sade's powerful imagination and courage allows the reader to enter into a human destiny with respect and responsibility. Ethics, as he writes, "takes courage and imagination" (1998, 12). The moral breakthrough is reached through an exploration of self-knowledge that is free from narcissism and moralism. Following Hillmann, Moore states something very similar to what has been recognized by Cowan. These forms of perversions have the strength of de-personalizing the ego and regrounding the person (1998, 157).
4 Parenthetically, in *Phenomenology of Perception* (1962) Merleau-Ponty describes consciousness and body as two poles that mark out the existence of the same object; similarly in *Nature and Spirit* (*Natur und Geist*) (2002) Husserl considers Spirit and Nature as two poles of the same flow. We can imagine it as a cone in which there are different layers which are moved upward and downward by different currents of forces. This force that describes the unity of the different strata and constitutes the mind-body unit is named the intentional arc by Merleau-Ponty (1962, 136, 157). To summarize it, the intentional arc is that which "brings about the unity of the senses, of intelligence, of sensibility and motility" (1962, 136). In Husserl what is called "practical intentionality" can be compared to Merleau-Ponty's intentional arc which describes the arc of unity formed by consciousness and body. On the one hand consciousness formalizes and transforms into meanings the matter of the body and its sedimentations; on the other, consciousness points to what pertains to

the body (1962, 130, 133, 137). While the body holds a form of intentionality that is sheer affectivity and follows the flow of life (1962, 157), consciousness transforms this affectivity into a meaning that is there for us. For example, speech is a psychological coming to existence; it represents the body of thought (182). These two sides are of course necessary to each other; the one would not be fulfilled without the other. We would not be able to fully feel a need if we were not able to give a meaning to it. That is the problem that arises in sexual activity, especially in the case of perversions; the drive is not fully formalized and transformed into meanings because there is a level of the intentional arc that tends to block the material drive.

5 The reorganization is made possible because of time. As Husserl wrote in C-1 17 4, there are least three senses of time: egoless and pretemporal, immanent experience, and world-time constituted through our acts. Taking care not to confuse the latter with the two previous modes of time can aid us in grasping the phenomenological idea of time as living present (*lebendige Gegenwart*, Hua XIV, 45, 301; Hua XXV, 25, 26), which Husserl described as "an ongoing filling of protentions and retentions. It is a creative primal presenting." Time is a point that we can describe as a here and now and it cannot be confused with our way of feeling this point because it is pre-egoic. If we do that we would fall in a form of psychologism that would bend this present egoless structure to our psychological interpretation of it. Neither can we explain time as a cause and effect bond, because otherwise we would bend time to our logical way of seeing it and we would not see it as Being unfolding itself in front of us. Hence in order to avoid to fall into the pitfall of a dualistic interpretation of existence, we need to consider time as a here-now wherein the fusion of immanent egoless experiences is constituted through acts.

Bibliography

Barney, R. (2008). "Eros and Necessity in the Ascent of the Cave," *Ancient Philosophy*, vol. 28, 1–15.

Carman, T. (1999). "The Body in Husserl and Merleau-Ponty." *Philosophical Topics,* vol. 27, no. 2, 205–226.

Cowan, L. (1982). *Masochism. A Jungian View.* Ann Arbor: Spring Publications Inc.

Ferrarello, S. (2015). *Husserl's Ethics and Practical Intentionality*. London/New York: Bloomsbury.

First, M. B. (2014). "DSM-5 and Paraphilic Disorders," *American Academy Psychiatry Law*, vol. 42, no. 2, 191–201.

Husserl, E. (1983). *Ideas Pertaining to a Pure Phenomenology and to a Phenomenological Philosophy*, (ed. Kersten, F.). The Hague: Martinus Nijhoff.

Husserl, E. (2001). *Analyses Concerning Passive and Active Syntheses. Lectures on Transcendental Logic*, (trans. Steinbock, A. J.). Dordrecht: Kluwer Academic Publishers.

Husserl, E. (2001). *Logical Investigations*, (trans. Findlay, J. N. and ed. Moran, D.). London and New York: Routledge.

Husserl, E. (2002). *Natur und Geist. Vorlesungen Sommersemester 1919*, (ed. Weiler, M.). Dordrecht: Kluwer Academic Publishers.

Krueger, J. W. (2006). "The Varieties of Pure Experience: William James and Kitaro Nishida on Consciousness and Embodiment." *William James Studies*, vol. 1, 1–37.

Merleau-Ponty, M. (1962). *Phenomenology of Perception*, (trans. Smith, C.). London and New York: Routledge.

Moore, T. (1998). Dark Eros. Thompson, CT: Spring Publications.

Nagel, T. (1997). "Sexual Perversion," in Philosophical Perspectives on Sex and Love, 105–12, (ed. Stewart, R. M.). New York: Oxford University Press.

Sartre, J.-P. (1956). *Being and Nothingness* (trans. Hazel, E.). New York: Washington Square Press.

Sartre, J.-P. (1972). "The Self-Alienation of the Lover's Freedom," in *Sexual Love and Western Morality*, (ed. Verene, D. P.). New York: Harper and Row.

4

INTRODUCTION TO THE PHENOMENOLOGY OF PHILIA

Introduction

Is intimate experience a form of lived-experience to which we can give our actual consent? Do intimate bonds allow us to discover something new about ourselves? If so, how can we choose what we want to know? This chapter will investigate the lived-experience of intimacy and its ethical implications in relation to the problem of consent within the constitution of our psychological and moral identity.

In order to investigate this phenomenon, in the first part of the chapter I will focus on what Husserl calls lower and higher spirit (which we already examined in Chapter 2), and wakeful ego; while in the second part I will describe the genetic constitution of intimate bonds as well as the generative web of instincts, habits, and values with which intimate love expresses itself as a bond-forming force.

Lower and Higher Spirit

As we saw in the previous chapter, for Husserl the volitional body (Hua-Mat 4, 186) is a layer between the spiritual and material parts of our body. (Ideas II, 1989, Chapters 1 to 3; Husserl, 2002, 185–186). For this reason, it cannot be considered exclusively either a spiritual or a material whole; thereby, if one wants to understand how a sexual subject engages with the world, one needs to inquire into the realm of the "material spirit," that is the several degrees that—from the most material to the most ethereal—explain how the spirit engages with its natural layers.

To clarify this point it is helpful to refer to the sixth chapter of volume 37 of Husserliana in which Husserl describes *Geist* (the spirit) as a spirit of inferior and superior qualities (Hua XXXVII, 107). The inferior spirit represents the layer of lower affection, which I will describe in the second part of this chapter as the generative web of drives, desires, instincts, and habits. On this level the spirit is not yet an ego; instead, it is the flow of that which is primitive and original. This is the level of the spirit that is the closest to Nature. "Nature" here signifies an underlying whole that expresses ontological lawfulness (Hua XXXVII, 103) and a universal interconnectedness that cannot be intellectually understood but only felt through the sphere of affections (*Gemüt*).

On this level spirit is a whole of primal affections and instincts that come to be continuously sedimented as habitus[1] in the realm of passivity or subpersonal spirit (Hua XXXIX, 422, 483). As Moran (2011) remarks, it is by means of habits that meaning (as in *Sinnhaftigkeit*) and sense (Husserl's *Sinnesgestalten*) are constituted, and therefore personal characters are determined and sedimented on many different levels. Motivations, interests, and volitions flow from this sedimentation. In *Ideas II*, sections 54–56 Husserl connects "habit" (*Gewohnheit*) with "the fundamental lawfulness of spiritual life" (*Die Motivation als Grundgesetz der geistigen Welt*). Indeed, habit functions as a form of primitive "association" (*Assoziation*) through which the lower spirit sediments its basic character and accordingly the core of its motivational life. "The similar motivates the similar under similar circumstances" (quoted in Moran, Hua IV, 225; En. tr. 236).

Motivation is not something originally connected to volitions or an ego's ends, because original motivation is egoless and grounded in the organic material level. As a matter of fact motivation is a passive force that irrationally or pre-rationally moves the hyletic flow, affecting the biological body and turning it into a subject.

"The first law" (Hua IV, 222; En. tr. 234) of motivation is rooted in this continuous tendency to be. We are motivated because our biological body (*Körper*, that is, a body that is not ours yet) encounters nature and feels an evidence that grounds axiological, aesthetic, practical, or theoretical values. Struck by this flow, the Body (Hua XXXVII, 114) feels an immediate rightness that it experiences as truth. This bodily (*Leibhaftig*) encountered truthfulness founds the value itself—or what is believed to be true—as an immediate hyletic datum. These beliefs, habits, affections do not entail any active position-taking, because they are the original core for the constitution of the ego. The encounter represents the birth of emotional consciousness (Hua XXXVII, 117); that is, the a priori condition and eidetic laws (Hua XXXVII 118, 115) for any correct act.

The superior spirit is the spirit that constitutes itself as an I and participates in the constitution of its meaning. On this level, hyletic sexual drives and sheer instincts are owned by an I that can clarify its core of habitus and actions (Hua XXXVII, 104). In *Analyses* Husserl writes:

> The part "demands" the whole—something uniform awakens something else that is uniform, which is not yet at all constituted as a unity explicitly for itself; and it does not demand the whole by a pure and simple awakening, but rather by a co-connected "expectation," by the demand as coexisting as co-belonging to the unity. Even the force of this apperceptive expectation increases with the number of "instances"—or with habit, which amounts to the same thing.
>
> *(Hua XI, 190; En. tr. 240)*

As the passage shows, the uniform egoless matter awakens other uniform matter that is not yet unity; this awakening generates a co-connected chain of expectations that will eventually organize into a self-assembling system which the subject will own and adapt to a meaning. According to Husserl there are essential self-organizing laws that order matter into a uniform and homogeneous core that one might call whole; this whole obeys natural necessity or the immediate sense of rightness that strikes the body and triggers its reaction to give meaning. In this way the body transforms a flow of indistinct hyletic data into a homogeneous unit (Hua XXXVII, 102). It is the transition between these two levels that opens the door to what we call intimacy. Indeed, on the lower level subjective bodies are motivated in the sense that they are mere functions of the uniform matter of drives and instincts for varied forms of consciousness (Hua XXXVII, 101): emotive, logical, and practical (*et alia*) consciousness. At this level motivation has to do with what the ego considers it worthwhile to do. The lawfulness is determined in an intelligible sense, through which the motivational force turns from something hyletic and egoless into something reflexive and personal. On the higher level the subject awakes and becomes aware of what its uniform matter wants to pursue. Being aware of the lawful interconnection of motivation creates a space of intimacy in which the subject can operate while being close to its organic matter.

In the next section I will first describe how caring love runs through the lower and higher spirit in connecting the degrees of our material and spiritual life and then I will describe the space of intimacy that this form of love discloses.

Love and the Constitution of the Spirit

Husserl considers love to be a sentiment that entails a true awakening (Husserl Ms. E III 4, 12b), because it is through intimate love that one can gather a privileged access to our lower and higher spirit; hence to our egoless and egoic life.

Through love the lower and higher levels of spirit can be awoken and connected with each other; first through desires, then through a volitional acknowledgment of their meanings and values. On the lower level Husserl describes desires as not simply a "turning toward" but a "striving after" (*Analyses*, ibid., 282). "Desire," he writes,

> is a tendency that occurs in the way that both passivity as well as activity are carried out, everywhere an intentionality of feeling in the mode of striving ... [and] has its positivity and negativity, like feeling in general. Its fulfillment is a relaxation that results from realizing [the striving, etc.], in the change into the corresponding joy of fulfillment: At root, joy lies in the arrival of what was lacking.
>
> *(Ibid., 282)*

Desire is a tendency that connects passive and active layers of our actions; in that sense it is considered as belonging to our intentionality of feeling (Ferrarello, 2015). The fulfillment of this intentional striving (or the lack of it) leads to a sense of joy that gives (or subtracts) meanings and values to the experiential goal that was felt as desirable by us. From this perspective desire seems to represent one of the vessels that leads our lower drives to the shores of our higher spirit.

A better understanding of the intentional structure of this tendency can be attained if we look at the crossroads of intentionalities I presented in Chapter 2: the intersection between passive syntheses (lower material level) and active intentionality (higher subjective level) as they are informed by practical intentionality (awakening). Husserl in fact calls intentionality of feeling that mode of striving that aims at a contact between passivity, i.e., what is not yet subjective, and activity, i.e., the meaning-giving activity through which we discover our being a subject.[2] In this encounter joy arises as the outcome of two intentions, whose structure is different from one another. On the one hand, the passive syntheses are egoless material fusions between affectant and affected which take place according to a principle of homogeneity[3] (Experience and Judgment, Analyses, Formal and Transcendental Logic) and their "hidden teleology" (C, 70; K, 71) moves toward a sense that still needs to be recognized and unfolded. On the other hand, when the subject is awoken by these syntheses, it activates itself in giving a meaning to that sense. Oftentimes the problematic aspect of this process lies in the communication between lower (passive syntheses) and higher spirit (meaning activity position). The awakening (practical intention) in fact invites the almost awake organic body, still involved in the ongoing activity of passive syntheses, to take responsibility for these passive syntheses (desires, drives, emotions) and interpret them in the right way. Since the synthetic process is an unstoppable one, which goes on even when we are in fact dead, the ability to take responsibility for that vast realm is an almost infinite task and demands a great deal of humility. As Hart noted (1992, 231), through the active recognition of passive syntheses we displace our self within a territory that we did not yet know. Our self is seen as a first other that we want (or not) to recognize and let harmonize with the space of world in which we just woke up. This first encounter between passive syntheses and active intentionality is what I call intimacy and it is what opens the individual to the vertical stream of love. The first intimate bond we create is with our passive selves and then others; this connection is established through our ability to be awake and create a contact between our lower and higher spirit. The next section will focus on the structure of wakefulness and the ego's volitional stance in relation to it.

Wakefulness and Consent

Since love among all the sentiments involves a true awakening (Husserl Ms. E III 4, 12b), love is also that connecting force that brings self-assembling matter to unity; this unity can be interpreted as individuals' or groups' identity. Through the gradual (Hua XXXII, 36) awakening my I is affected by passive syntheses and starts acquiring knowledge in relation to its lower matter. On this level the volitional body is called to take a position of validation that might result in the acceptance or refusal of what is offered to it. This is the primitive act of moral identity performed by the subject.

Issuing from the passive perceptual situation, letting oneself be determined such that one has a judicative position and then has a judicative determination. Thus, we also understand why in practice, judging and conviction become equivalent expressions. We will see shortly that this position-taking or this group of position-takings that occur here are completely non-independent from the standpoint of intentionality, namely, insofar as they presuppose the occurrences of passive doxa. Let us note in advance that these position-takings, this validation and its transformations, further, are not to be confounded with other modes of comportment by the ego that belong to the sphere of judgment, especially not with active explication, colligation, comparison, differentiation, and the like—all of the operations to which we are indebted for the logical forms of different state-of-affairs.

(Analyses, 93/53)

As is evident from this passage, validations are the most primitive acts through which one allows oneself to take a specific shape as a person. Whenever we take a position that validates or not the passive syntheses of affections, whether this validation will result in the acceptance of external interpretation of our character or in the refusal of the values projected upon us, every validation is going to shape our personality. In the next sections I will go deeper in the details of how drives, instincts, and habits interact with this act of validation, acceptance, and consent. It is important to remark here that the volitional body allows the transition between lower and higher spirit, passive and active intentionality through an act of consent, "a yes or no," that meaningfully is going to shape our intimate life and what we are in relation to ourselves and the society in which we live. As Husserl writes "the realm of activity is *eo ipso* a realm of free volitional activity" (*Analyses*, 283/11). On the level of active volitions we decide how our living body will interact with its matter and give a meaning to it, on the level of passive volitions our body decides which passive matter is going to affect our awakening and how to handle that responsibility.

The noetic Yes and No, however, arise from taking a position specifically as judging. (...) Here, of course, this correlate is the noematic "valid" or "invalid" arising in the objective sense; it occurs in the objective sense with the character of being declared valid or invalid by the ego.

(Analyses, 94)

The consent (*Zustimmung, Einverständnis*)[4] comes from a level of volitional activity in which the just-awoken ego recognizes the values and meanings that were passively motivating its acts as material syntheses.[5] The mark of interest— which I was discussing above—that characterizes a powerful sentiment like love consists exactly in the ability of the I to be in that flow that connects lower and higher spirit. The organic syntheses through the active participation of the volitional body transform into values, judgments, and finally a social stance the interest mark proper to their subjective presence (Hua XXXXII, 192).

Love, Consent, and its Ambiguity

This description provides some clues as to how difficult it can be to define the consent from the part of the volitional body. In fact, the ownership we can claim over our body will be always limited to the point of awakening in which our ego finds itself whenever the irritations arise; our awakening always uncovers a limited space of passive matter.

For example, educations, habits, the geographic and social map of our life, tends to generate in us an habitual form of awakening that does not cause too much distress because it always takes place in the same area of our life. Yet, when something extraordinary happens to us, such as falling in love, our ordinary space of awakening is expanded to something new, which seems familiar, intriguing, and frightening at the same time.

The famous Ovidian "amo et odi" summarizes this universal feeling, for which love forces us to awake to something new and often hideous about ourselves because it sheds light on parts of us that we are not always willing to visit or simply that we do not want to know.

Hence, the consent that follows any validation generates in us a sense of responsibility that is proportional to the matter that we decide to own; its meanings and values will be always limited to the level of understanding we can hold in relation to that space of awakening. There are cases in which people fall in love because the beloved one is capable of making them free to attend to an unknown new area of their life; whether this area is full of darkness and flaws or light and good qualities, that new understanding will be in any case valuable because it will have the worth of mending previous wounds that otherwise would remain buried into the sedimented layers of their passive life. Love is a vital and somewhat brutal force that awakens us in a place that is not familiar for us, but at the same time is particularly important because it can foster our spiritual (lower and higher) growth. It is in fact through this force that we are given a larger view on what we are. On the other hand, the feeling of love shows us that our level of consent to it as a disclosure to an intimate space will never be fully informed and weary of its consequences. We can only sense what is important for us and what we want to be respected in us, but mostly our consent will be a process of ongoing discovery that can even lead to a direction that conflicts with our physical or psychological well-being.

The next chapter will be entirely focused on the problem of forced intimacy and validations. A full consent always evolves through an arc of time that cannot be synchronistic to the event that takes place; it often involves a long and sometimes painful process of discovery that will necessarily be asynchronous to the event of awakening. The value/meaning-giving activity, in fact, will never be exhausted in the moment itself because the synthetic matter is generally too wide to be comprised in only one validation.

Instincts, Habits, and Brutal Love

As emerged in the previous section, the primal bond of intimate love that bridges lower and higher spirit is due to a primal self-assembling and synthetic force that we can call love; this connecting force opens a space of intimacy through which the human being can regain contact with their passive matter. In this section, I will examine the genetic and generative[6] components that belong to this force. As Hart noted, Husserl once claimed that "love is a chief problem of phenomenology," by which he meant that love "is a universal problem for phenomenology because it embraces the depths and heights of intentionality as a driving and productive force" (1992, 225).

In this analysis love is not taken as a static category only, but as a genetic and transformative one as well. As mentioned above, the lowest sensuous roots of love comprise desires, instincts,[7] impulses,[8] drives, while the heights of love comprise meanings, values, and higher feelings. Lowest and highest roots of love tend to move in two opposite directions since the former tend to irritate the ego to the point of its awakening, and the latter builds around the ego a psychic armor that we might call "personality" that turns the ego into a semi-sleeping, static being. Both sides of this force are a necessary bridge to connect the lower and higher spirit. As Lee remarks (1993, 166), the lowest roots of our being are original affections (*Uraffektionen*) that originally awaken us and call us to be. They are the organic matter that manifests itself as being there for the ego (Hua-Mat VIII, 351). "Original affection is an instinct, thus a kind of empty striving still lacking the presentation of a goal" (Hua–Mat VIII, 253). These affections present a hidden kind of intentionality, which has its direction but is not yet cognitively explicit. As Husserl writes:

> Here the word "instinct" is used in an unusually broad sense, first of all for each drive-intentionality [Triebintention], which originally is not yet disclosed in its sense. Instincts in the usual sense relate to remote, originally hidden goals, in a chain of partial drives aiming at these goals and serving the preservation of the species, or, as the case may be, the self-preservation of the individual of the species.
>
> *(Ms. E III 10, 6a)*

The lowest roots of love have an intention that is not known to the subject and is not yet owned by it. That is why love is often described in poetry as a force that takes us—Dante for example wrote "Love, so swift to grasp a tender heart."[9] We do not choose to love, it is love that chooses us and moves us toward directions that we cannot know immediately, and even less control. The intentional movement of this sensuousness seems to be aimed at self-preservation; whenever we love someone we confide in eternity, or as Sartre put it, we hope that our thinghood can finally come to existence through the regard of the Other. In that sense instincts are our deeper connection to the hidden goal that regulates our survival. Husserl assigns instincts an intentional quality which, even if not comparable to the active intentionality described in his *Logical Investigations* or *Ideas* because lacking of a referring quality (*Beziehung auf*), is still intentional since it forms a tension toward something through associations. Husserl describes the instinctive intention in these terms:

> Unity of the process of filling of intention, and this itself is the telos, namely, that the instinctive intention which in a unified way from the start heads towards this interpenetration of intentionality and its releasement and is fulfilled as something unified not in a single phase but in an ongoing achievement (Tun).
>
> *(C 16 IV, 14; see Lee, 1993, 109)*

The instinctive intention triggers a process of ongoing achievements for which the *telos* (goal) that moves the affectant and the affected of the synthesis can be fulfilled because of the act that the subject awoken by those syntheses decides to take. Instincts and drives have the strength to move upward from the depth of our organic life to the activity of our decisions.

It is when our instinct emerges to the surface of our active decision that an opposite force takes shape, that of the habits. Indeed, when instincts tend to emerge always in the same locus and to drive us toward the same validation, they can easily become habitualized and constitute a stable layer; an example of it can be the instinct of hunger that arises always around lunch time.

On this level instincts and habits compete with each other. The repetition of validated instincts become habits; while the directionality of instinct opens to new territories and it draws a vertical trajectory because it starts from the lower primordial affections and travels up to higher feelings, the directionality of habits is horizontal and tend to fix fleeting instincts into stable sense-meanings and values. When habits and instincts conflict in love, Husserl warns us:

> There is indeed a danger here. Because an absolute ought and an absolute value is only what it is as an absolute statement, in absolute love; and a love which would be mechanized, is no love. Although love becomes habitualized, it is only real and actual in active exertion.
>
> *(Husserl, Ms. E III 4, 12b)*

Real love is actual only in active exertion; when love is mechanized, constrained, and shaped by habits, love ceases to be that absolute ought that defines its essence. Naturally, love, like any other lower feeling, can be habitualized; when that happens part of its brutal force is lessened. Yet, since caring intimate love "embraces the depths and heights of intentionality," it cannot dwell in only one of two positions for too long if it is actively exerted; so if it gets stuck on the lower or higher level it means that its power is not fully exerted. Whenever habits inevitably emerge from the repetition of instincts, love frees itself through breaking those habits and freeing new sensuous lower matter; whenever instincts repeatedly erupt without allowing the constitution of stable patterns, love normalizes the instincts through affections and constancy needs. Love is actual when it shocks and awakes the ego to a new intimate bond within the richness of its sensuous matter. Any ego lives a necessary double life between free instincts and sedimented habits; on the one hand instincts awake its being to the matter that the ego needs to own in that given moment as a responsible being within a community, on the other hand habits shape its personality according to the content of its sensuous matter and it is through that personality that it can live in the real world. As Husserl recognizes I am not only the I that awakes in that moment of time under the irritating pressure of its drives, but I am also a cycle of habitualities that start building out of awakenings. The habits have the goal to actualize my ability to be and allow me to come into existence by fulfilling my qualities and fine-tuning my capabilities. On the other hand they prevent me from exploring all the drives that are blossoming in different directions.

Husserl wrote:

> The personal Ego constitutes itself not only as a person determined by *drives* (...) but *also as a higher, autonomous, freely acting* Ego, in particular one guided by *rational motives* (...). Habits are necessarily formed, just as much with regard to originally instinctive behavior (...) as with regard to free behavior. To yield to a drive establishes the drive to yield: habitually. Likewise, to let oneself be determined by a value-motive and to resist a drive establishes a tendency (a "drive") to let oneself be determined once again by such a value-motive (...) and to resist these drives.
>
> *(Hua IV, 255; En. tr. 267)*

As this passage shows, at the level of passive syntheses the most effective motives might be those to which we do not attend and do not become habits (see Hua XI, 178 and Lee, 1993, 55). Whether we want it or not, our personality is determined by drives and on a higher level the choices that we make in relation to them. Hence, on a higher level the intimate bond that is established through love runs through validations that involve our volitional body, while on a lower level through instincts that escape our ability to consent. When an intimate bond is established, then our primary I emerges from the whole of instincts and drives that we decide to accept and explore; this whole of lower affections become recognizable through habitualizations and then active meanings that we decide to assign to the bundle of instincts that became visible through habits. In this always-new-I, we can see a number of capacities that we can accept or not, and it is through this acceptance that we participate in the flow of life as persons that can build an intimate life with themselves and others.[10] As Husserl writes, "As feeling is founded in the hyletic or the affective tonality [*Gefühlsmässigen*] of the hyle so the conative as response-form of the I is founded in the affective tonal" (Ms. E III 9, 16b).

While the intimacy disclosed by the lower level of instincts sheds light on the dark area of validity and consent because we cannot ever be fully aware of all our instincts; the higher level of caring intimate love which assigns meanings and values to the passive matter has the merit to bring awareness and a sense of interconnection. The interconnection is first between the lower and higher level of spirit and then between individuals. It is in this dimension of interconnectedness that the I comes to existence as a person. Human beings are in fact places of validity from which intimacy stems as founding force which interconnect different points of owning matter (the awoken ego) through acts of validation (Hua I, 54, 55, 62). In Husserl we can distinguish primordialness (*Urtümlichkeit*) as the primordialness of my, the mature, self-reflecting I (higher level), and the primordialness that, through the further questioning back (*Rückfrage*) and through the uncovering of the genesis, becomes reconstructed habitual primordialness (lower level), the primordialness of the "beginning" of constitutive genesis.

When I decide to be intimate with someone, first of all myself, I discover my self as being interconnected with another and since I am a living system I keep interpreting what am I in relation to the Other. Hence, intimacy is never given, created, or discovered once and for all, but it is a generative and participative concept; this means that my hidden past will always stand out in a dark horizon as impediment for true intimacy and at the same time a resource for its generative quality (C 13 III, 7; Lee, 1993, 28).

Men (*Menschen*) are in fact defined by Husserl as organic functioning elements (Hua-Mat IX, 170, 176) that do not belong solely to their monads but are parts of a larger whole. My genetic and lower life is not primordially mine; the awakening of my ego makes that life mine. The space of intimacy that that awakening unfolds makes my own functioning and validating system part of other systems. For Husserl, individuals are units of goals, values, and certitudes (Hua-Mat IX, 171) that relate to each other in a social community. I can grasp the interconnection of my space of intimacy with other spaces through my habitual I who can sediment layers that allow the reflecting I to grasp its own being. Human beings are *concreta* that relate to the whole of society as parts to a whole, and these parts are a whole on its turn. They can function independently of the whole-society, but as they explicate their task they form a whole with the society to which they belong. The way in which the wholes are formed is through love and the way in which these wholes are kept together is through a fluid access to intimacy.

Hence the individual is not an isolated monad in society. Everyone is responsible for what part of themself they bring into "one single universal coherence." The goals and the values that move each personal subject to action are inevitably interconnected to the values of others.

Conclusion

This chapter discussed first the lower and higher layers of the spirit in order to explain how the volitional body—the moral organ of our actions—validates the feelings that lead us to intimate love. In the chapter I showed how this body cannot be considered as belonging exclusively to material or immaterial layers; accordingly every decision it makes participate of lower and higher motives. It is under these lenses that the brutal force of love and the space of intimacy that it opens up was interpreted as a vertical feeling connecting lower and higher, material and immaterial layers of us; on a lower level love is a whole of drives, instincts, desires of which cannot have a firm hold because we do not own them. On this level in fact the subject is not even an ego yet, but is an ongoing chain of syntheses of the passive matter. On the higher level, love is a meaning and value-giving activity; it interprets the passive matter that is provided to it through the awakening of the I and validates it according to specific meanings and values that shed lights on what that person actually is. The light shed on these layers form a space of intimacy through which the person can come in contact with parts of itself that were unexplored or not yet revealed. The bonding force of love represents a unique opportunity for us to become closer to our factual existence. This involves that on the one hand intimacy will discloses a dark place where the sensuous egoless generative web of syntheses build a concreteness that might eventually take its own shape into meanings and values constitutive for the identity and sense of reality that a person feels to live in.; on the other hand intimacy represents a retrospective reconstruction of the layers of the known intimate life as it appears to be sedimented in the habitual layers of an I. The former kind of intimacy lays the foundation for a valid, but yet dark, space in which the I can come into existence, the latter recognizes the interconnection between the layers that belong to that validity as a founding core around which life, the habitual one, constitutes itself as a meaningful vital flow.

Notes

1 The terms usually employed by Husserl to express habits are: *Gewohnheit, Habitus, Habitualität, das Habituelle,* or the Greek *hexis*; sometimes he also uses the verbal phrase "possession" of (*Besitz*), the "having" (*Habe*) of a skill, or "habits of thought" (*Denkgewohnheiten*). Husserl uses "*Habitus*" to express the concept of "demeanor" or "comportment" as combined with human personal abilities.

2 See for example, Hua XXXI, 8:

> These values determinations are not the arbitrarily varying characters of feeling, they are predicates, that is, elements that are identifiable; but the sources from which the objectivation for these predicates are drawn are the feelings and the contents of them accruing to the matters in questions. But in the final analysis, one must distinguish here between the intentionality of feeling itself, and the objectivating—be it passive or in higher level active—the objectivating that objectivates the contents arising in the intentionality of feeling and that makes use of them in order to constitute new predicate layers with respect to matters that are constituted in other ways.

3 See: Experience and Judgment, section 16, 75; Analyses Concerning Passive and Active Syntheses, section 26.

4 Hua, XXXVIIII, Beilage XVII, 223:

> Treten in der A1-Periode mir fremde Menschen gegenüber, sich als Menschen normal ausweisend, so sind sie Menschen, die ihrerseits Erfahrung von dieser selben A-Welt haben, in Bezug auf sie personale Einheiten sind wie ich; und für mich sind sie als das im Einverständnis gegeben und ich für sie; Hua XXXXII, 276: "Und da ich eines und das andere wei., werde ich mich entsprechend bestimmen lassen und nicht ohne Weiteres zustimmen, nicht ohne Weiteres ablehnen.

5 Hua XXXXII, 192:

> Und in dieser Hin-sicht bin ich dafür interessiert, dass meine Urteile anderen als richtig gelten, dass sie von ihnen anerkannt, in Zustimmung übernommen werden und eventuell auch meine Begründungen dafür. Selbst wo ich schon einsehe, dass sie falsch und die Begründungen untriftig sind, mag ich interessiert sein daran, dies anderen zu verdecken und mir den sozialen Wert des klugen Mannes zu erhalten. Hier ist nicht das Urteil selbst durch einen Wert des Urteils motiviert, sondern Wert ist hier, dass mein Urteil Anderen als richtiges gelte, dass sie mir zustimmen und mich für einen wahr Urteilenden halten, mich als das beurteilen.

6 I mean generative as transformative, see Steinbock, A. (1995). *Home and Beyond: Generative Phenomenology after Husserl.*

7 The study of instincts is not only a genetic concern. He touched on this topic in the fifth of the *Logical Investigations* (see Hua XIX/1, 409; see Lee, 1993, 43ff.)

8 See for example, on the theme of impulses in Husserl, *Alter*, (2001), 9.

9 Dante's verses:

> Love, so swift to grasp a tender heart, /is what made him want my once fair form/wrenched from me with much yet felt offense. /Love, which won't let beloved stay apart/struck me with such strong enjoyment for this man that, as you see, it has not yet abandoned me.

10 Hua XIV, 378:

> I am not only an actual but I am also a habitual ego, and habituality signifies a certain egoic possibility, an "I can" or "I could," or "I would have been able to," and this ability become actual refers to ego-actualities, to actual ego-experiences; that is, as actualization of ability. In a word, I am (and without this would not be an I, I can not think of myself otherwise), an ego of capacities.

Bibliography

Hart, J. (1992). "Entelechy in Transcendental Phenomenology." *American Catholic Philosophical Quarterly*, vol. 66, no. 2, 189–212.

Husserl, E. (1988). *Vorlesungen über Ethik und Wertlehre. 1908–1914*, (ed. Melle, U.). The Hague: Kluwer Academic Publishers.

Husserl, E. (2001a). *Analyses Concerning Passive and Active Syntheses. Lectures on Transcendental Logic*, (trans. Steinbock, A. J.). Dordrecht: Kluwer Academic Publishers.

Husserl, E. (2001b). *Logical Investigations*, (trans. Findlay, J. N. and ed. Moran, D.). London and New York: Routledge.

Husserl, E. (2002). *Natur und Geist. Vorlesungen Sommersemester 1919*, (ed. Weiler, M.). Dordrecht: Kluwer Academic Publishers.

Husserl, E. (2006). *Späte Texte über Zeitkonstitution (1929–1934). Die C-Manuskripte*, (ed. Lohmar, D.). New York: Springer.

Husserl, E. (2012). *Einleitung in die Philosophie. Vorlesungen 1916–1919*, (ed. Jacobs, H.). Dordrecht: Springer.

Lee, N. (1993). *Edmund Husserl's Phänomenologie der Instinkte*. Dordrecht: Springer.

Moran, D. (2011). "Edmund Husserl's Phenomenology of Habituality and Habitus." *Journal for the British Society of Phenomenology*, vol. 42, 53–77.

Steinbock, A. (1995). *Home and Beyond: Generative Phenomenology after Husserl*. Evanston: Northwestern University Press.

5

FORCED INTIMACY

Introduction

In this chapter I will focus on the case in which a space of intimacy is opened up without one's consent and in doing this, I will apply Husserl's genetic method on what Koestenbaum calls "existential sexuality." The chapter will be divided into two parts. The first part will follow up on the description of practical intentionality and the genesis of intimacy provided in the previous chapters. The second part will analyze the link between sexuality and intimacy to show how the genetic character of intimacy informs the passive and active choices that constitute one's sexual identity. The goal of the chapter is to describe how and why intimacy can become a space that opens to us despite our consent and unfolds uncontrollable meanings.

Existential Sexuality

This section will investigate the teleological and recursive structure of existential sexuality, which I will read as being defined by the passive and active layers of the decisions people habitually make in their intimate lives. In my opinion, existential intimacy is the most relevant characteristic of the recursive structure of existential sexuality because its fluid nature provides the key to understanding our sexual facticity and the meanings we assign to it.

I borrowed the term *existential sexuality* from Koestenbaum, whose therapeutic approach is directly influenced by existentialism and Husserl's phenomenology. In his *Existential Sexuality* he defines existential sex as the "chosen sex; it is the sex life that an individual has chosen authentically.... There's no law that says life must include love.... Our freedom is total" (1974, 10).

According to Koestenbaum, our sexuality is existential in the moment in which it acquires a meaning for us; the meaning comes from the awareness of our decision. Love is not the law around which we build sexual identity; we have absolute freedom in our sexual facticity. He continues: "Meaning stands for integration, meaning refers to total life and to the fulfillment of its potential.... [E]xistential or meaningful sex is sex experienced as an integral part of a beautiful life" (1974, 8). "Choosing to cope" (1974, 12) is the first step that leads to the meaning and the beauty of our sexual existence.

The Recursive Structure of Sexual Existence

The problem that any existential choice entails is directly connected to the structure of our being. As Sartre remarks (1956), we are factual beings, meaning that we are part of a reality that we do not fully understand and at the same time we are meanings that we continuously construct. Making a choice about our existence means, as Koestenbaum writes, "being awake to each situation" (1974, 13). Our receptivity, as McDowell (1996) and Husserl (2001) remarked, is such that we often construct meanings without being able to attend to them consciously; the meanings that define our lives are often meaningless and even invasive for us. Although these meanings represent who we factually are, usually we are not fully aware of the determining power they have on our lives.

For example, people involved in extramarital affairs may realize that they are in an affair only when the latter relationship negatively affects the harmony of the former one (Zapien, 2017). Before that realization they might not feel they were part of the category "affair" because the decisions they made were grounded mostly in their passive and receptive life. Their new sexual identity was shaped without their being aware of it. Being awake to one's meaning is an important step toward the constitution of a meaningful existential construct that can shape one's facticity in a way that can be recognized as authentic. In *The Transformation of Intimacy*, Giddens states that

> a pure relationship is one in which external criteria have become dissolved: the relationship exists solely for whatever rewards that

relationship can deliver. In the context of the pure relationship, trust can be mobilised only by a process of mutual disclosure.

(1992, 40)

An intimate relationship is a relationship of an active choice of intimacy that is made by partners who decide to be close to themselves as individuals and to each other as related individuals.

Sexual existential freedom lies exactly in the decision to be awake and attend to the constitution of one's sexual identity. As Koestenbaum notes: "In reality a human being is a free consciousness; activity and passivity are free role choices. The meaning of sexual activity is not preordained by human anatomy but is created by free choices of liberated men and women" (1974, 93). Realizing that we are free from inappropriate moral constraints and social constructions would enable us to meaningfully invite passive meaning to become active.

Koestenbaum calls the space of this absolute freedom *transcendental*. By that the author is referring to the space of the original constitution of meanings. It is in this space in fact that "consciousness is prior to sex and that consciousness is asexual. The sexualization of consciousness is a free decision and a free construction" (1974, 86). In this space the asexual free consciousness decides to become meaningful. According to Koestenbaum:

> A therapeutic relationship, like existential love, is "transcendental." It is a relationship that exists on the level of pure consciousness... . It is a mind-to-mind encounter and not solely a feeling or emotional experience.... He perceives his love now as an object that must be lived. That distance from an emotion is a key to understanding existential love.
>
> *(1974, 25)*

Transcendental is the space opened up by the encounter of practical, passive, and active intention. As a space that describes the condition of the possibility for the sexual experience to be such, this space can be grasped through the awakening of passive matter into a now that acquires a meaning through active intention. This space is what I call intimacy, which I will describe in what follows. As we saw from Chapter 5, practical intention is that intention in which the subject as a just-awoken ego decides to own in the now the passive contents of its body and validates that content matter of active meaning-giving. The transcendental is precisely the space disclosed by the crossing of these three different qualities of intentions, which operate in a space of absolute freedom where the individual discovers the matter and accordingly the meanings that determine the sense of its own facticity. This space of transcendental (i.e., condition of possibility for a meaning) freedom is the space in which real intimacy between the subject and its own world is disclosed.

In a beautiful passage in *Being and Nothingness*, Sartre writes:

> As soon as I am referred to myself because I must await myself in the future, then I discover myself suddenly as the one who gives the meaning to the alarm clock ... the one finally who makes the values exist in order to determine his action by their demands. I emerge alone and in anguish confronting the unique and original project which constitutes my being.... I do not have nor can I have recourse to any value against the fact that it is I who sustains values in being. Nothing can ensure me against myself.... I have to realize the meaning of the world and of my own essence.
>
> *(1956, 39)*

According to Sartre, one discovers one's facticity through the free awakening of the I rising from the nothingness of Being.

I would call the dimension that both Koestenbaum and Sartre described in these passages, intimacy. It is in this space disclosed by an act of transcendental freedom that one acquires a space of absolute closeness with oneself and/or others whom one encounters in this original realm. This space of constitution of meanings connects one's passive layers of facticity with active existential ones. Indeed, it is in this space, as Sartre wrote, that "I have to realize the meaning of the world and of my own essence." In this space my facticity awakes and is moved to decide how close I want to be to what I really am and what I am becoming.[1] Hence, I consider intimacy the space from which my passive facticity and my active meaning-bestowing decisions stem in the definition of my being in the world as a sexual creature. As Koestenbaum wrote: "This transcendental closeness is more intimate than if it were sexual" (1974, 25). The transcendental closeness in which we constitute the meaning of our passive and active sexual existence is what I call intimacy.

As Sartre wrote:

> My existence in the midst of the world becomes the exact correlate of my transcendence-for-myself since my independence is

absolutely safeguarded.... Thus I am reassured.... My facticity is saved. It is no longer this unthinkable and insurmountable given which I am fleeing; it is that for which the Other freely makes himself exist; it is as an end which he has given to himself.... My existence is because it is given a name. I am because I give myself away.

(1956, 258)

I am because I can choose how close I want to be to myself; in doing that I disclose myself to the Other or—in Sartre's terms—"I give myself away." My facticity is saved because the passive layers that constitute it can finally acquire a meaning from my choice and the regard of the Other. My transcendental freedom is then used to inform an existential sexuality that is meaningful for me. The social construction that defines my sexual orientation ceases to be an empty category because it becomes a teleological recursive structure whose infinite unfolding of meanings changes while the essential given expressed in its facticity remains the same. Figuratively speaking, intimacy invites the exploration of this eternal maze in which the self is what we are chasing and mobile walls are the structure of which the self itself is made during its own chase.

Transcendental Intimacy

This section will describe the essential features that characterize transcendental intimacy and how they directly influence a person's sexual life. Poetry perhaps can capture the essence of this fluid and fleeting state of mind better than philosophy and explain how we can access intimacy.

Three contemporary Spanish poets agree that transcendental intimacy cannot be achieved spontaneously. While *intimacy is spontaneous, any reflection on intimacy detracts from spontaneity.* For García Montero, time is the synthetic medium that allows us to experience intimacy reflectively. According to García Montero, since poetry is a linguistic invention, a poet can never write about true intimacy; however, he or she can artificially trace its steps back to true intimacy through the reconstruction of a fictional time in which words contribute to the constitution of the intricate tangle of time and feelings from which intimacy stems. Similarly, in *Paraíso Manuscrito* (1982), Benítez Reyes considers intimacy a dialogue between words and memory. In this case intimacy does not refer to an abstract sense of time but to the precise act of recollection of past events in which we recover the feeling of being intimate. Finally, in *La Noche Junto al Álbum* (1980) Alvaro García points to the distant and intellectual sight as a practical device to get closer to the spontaneous feeling of intimacy. According to the poet, it is through this hybrid vision that one can re-create the intimate atmosphere in one's own poetry.

Hence, according to these poets, the transcendental dimension of intimacy can be re-evoked and explored through a use of reflective and transcendental time. This poetic reading of transcendental intimacy is consonant with Gendlin's philosophical and psychological description. In *Focusing* (1982), Gendlin reports a story told by a woman concerning her choice of remaining intimate to herself and her husband. In the story the woman was having dinner with her husband when he dropped some food on the tablecloth; the clumsiness of that small event was sufficient to trigger her rage. First she gives in to her rage, and then she decides to leave the table and go upstairs to her bedroom to practice focusing. This technique, influenced by Husserl's phenomenology, consists in letting the body speak its mind without forcing any meaning from it; through a free flow of words and ideas that prompt one's mind, the body is allowed to free some of its passive layers without committing to any active decision of interpretation. Thus, alone in her bedroom the wife let her mind run free while she was attending to the unfolding of her thoughts as a witness. Through this act of intellectual distancing in which she put herself in a modality of active dialogue with what she was feeling, she suddenly discovered the real reason for her anger. A new sense of deeper intimacy was restored. She was mad at her husband because during dinner he was celebrating his promotion, whereas her career was at a dead end because of her maternity.

Poetry, philosophy, and psychology seem to converge on the idea that the realm of transcendental or reflective intimacy can be explored and then enacted by a person's existential choices through recollection and distancing. In this short story, intimacy seems to be a two-layered dimension: the spontaneous passive one and the existential, active, and transcendental one. In the story, the passive layer of intimacy is represented by the argument between the spouses. Intimacy between the partners was broken because their factual lives were conflicting although they were not actively aware of that. The existential and active layer of intimacy is represented by the decision that the wife made to distance herself from the previous spontaneous intimacy and to be in dialogue with her reaction without imposing any moral judgment on her feeling. Her decision gave the couple a real opportunity to be truly close. The latter layer, the reflective one, allowed them to acquire a more meaningful and intimate relationship, open to new choices concerning their future together. That provided an opportunity for them to constitute a new meaning for their conjugal relationship. On the first passive lower layer intimacy spontaneously erupts as a space that transcends time and space; on the higher active layer it becomes an absolutely free space in which we can constitute meanings that will define our existence. On this second layer, we hold a decisional power. In this story the wife might have not been happy to discover her jealousy toward her husband's career, yet she used that realization to be close to herself and her husband's feelings.

Our passive life can easily disclose a gap that we cannot fill and from which we cannot come back. It is very common, in fact, to decide passively to negate closeness and choose a pregiven social construction that does not feel true to us but is socially accepted. In the story, being angry about clumsiness with the dishes is more socially acceptable than being envious and jealous of one's partner's professional success. Traditionally, women's goal has been to raise children whereas men have focused on their careers. It is difficult to participate in the teleological structure of a social construction in a way that we feel as truly teleological—that is, infinitely unfolding meanings for us—and recursive—that is, participative and actually changing our existence. The essence of our facticity always tries to connect spontaneously with us; whether we want to entertain a dialogue with it is a matter of transcendental and existential intimacy. The next section will go through the two layers of intimacy, the transcendental and the spontaneous, in relation to cases of forced intimacy.

Forced Intimacy

The interplay between spontaneous and transcendental layers of intimacy raises a relevant issue pertaining to consent and ownership of our intimate space. As a matter of fact intimacy does not stem from a willing choice, but from a forceful event[2] that opens a space of which we are called to be part even if we are not capable of fully seeing it. Intimacy opens up to us before we are able to give our consent to it; this is the reason why I characterize the layer of spontaneous intimacy as a forced one. Cases of forced intimacy can be numerous and not necessarily negative for the individual's psychological well-being. Witnessing an accident on the street, being moved by a scene of a movie in the theater, listening to a touching concert, are all cases in which we become intimate with other people, mostly strangers, despite our consent; we enter into an intersubjective space of intimacy in which a wave of feelings and emotions is spontaneously shared even if we are not ready to assign any meaning to it. In that case, spontaneous intimacy discloses a new intimate space in front of us without our consent; this space might be recollected and cognitively transformed into a place of intelligible meanings to which we can give our consent through transcendental intimacy. For example, after a concert one might decide to talk to the person sitting next to her and share a few words of appreciation about the music; after a car accident the witnesses might decide to cool down together the stress generated by the event. Any space of intimacy is originally disclosed by spontaneous syntheses of egoless matter, more simply by life as it flows in a number of affectant-affected fusions; this opening awakes our volitional body and then our ego which is called to take a position (the noetic yes/no, *Analyses*, 94/54) in relation to the passive matter (this is another way to describe the interconnection of passive, practical, and active intention). That yes or no is the primordial root of any consent; yet, it cannot be equated to a cognitive consent in which we decide calmly and in full awareness about what to do. Using a metaphor, the yes or no can be compared to the reaction that our body "decided"[3] to have if it saw an avalanche falling upon it; there is not so much time to decide, and yet our lower and higher spirit, that is our bodily drives, impulses and instincts and our personal habitual coping mechanisms and basic cognitions are all focused on making a decision. That is the range of freedom at disposal whenever we give our consent under the pressure of passive syntheses; the hyletic flow is so wide and powerful that it can in fact be compared to an avalanche. Even if we are only watching a movie, our senses are so busy in retrieving information that we are continuously called to decide what to own and what to leave to the process of sedimentations on passive layers.

For example, in watching a movie a meaningful memory of mine might be awoken and I might decide to own all the feelings that that memory stirs up in me as mine; at the same time it might happen that my body feels uncomfortable because of that wave of feelings and starts having reactions, like muscular contractions that I might not be ready to own or to fully recognize because my ego is awake elsewhere; maybe the contractions will reveal themselves later on in the form of headaches, although their meaning might not be completely understood.

These examples shed light on a positive form of forced intimacy, in which spontaneous intimacy reveals something meaningful and positive for our life. Things become far more complex when the space of intimacy is forced open because of actual violence. While in the positive form of spontaneous intimacy the forced event elicits a recollection that

is in a certain way peaceful and comforting, in the case of abrupt violence the interplay between transcendental and spontaneous intimacy is
less fluid.

For example, cases of acquaintance rape and/or other kinds of sexual
assault represent the condition for a deep conflict between spontaneous
and transcendental intimacy, as the forceful event—in this case rape—
discloses a spontaneous space of intimacy that the victim cannot be ready
to properly name and recollect. Indeed, the common places concerning
rape suggest that women are typically assaulted in dark alleys by strangers;
often in the case of acquaintance rape the truth instead is that the existence of an already intimate space between victim and assailant raises the
chances of assault and the difficulty of properly naming the event.[4]
When acquaintance rapes take place the familiarity of the intimate world
already shared with the assailant makes the victim incapable to assign a
fitting name for the irruption of the new layer of intimacy; the continuity with the habitual space of intimacy is such that the victim wants
to preserve the integrity of that space by renewing its habitual qualities.
In that sense, in some countries even language does not encourage a
proper recognition; for example, in numerous juridical contexts the
concept of "marital rape" did not exist legally.[5] By legal definition, "a
woman cannot be raped by her husband, since the 'crime' of rape is
ordinarily and legally defined as a forcing sexual intercourse on someone
other than the wife of the person accused."[6] When acquaintance rape
happens it is very difficult for the victim to assign a meaning to the act
that would feel true and respondent to the reality. Reading some interviews on the topic, it is very surprising to see that victims are often open
to accept marriage proposal by their assailants or to consider the rape as
premarital sex. This happens because the acceptance would renew the
continuity of the victim's previous intimate and social life; in this way
the spontaneous violence of the intimate act is recollected in a transcendental activity that does not recognize the change and therefore does
not adhere to the space disclosed by the spontaneous activity. Thus, in
this dynamic the actual intimacy with the spontaneous syntheses is precluded since the layer of transcendental intimacy is not anymore capable
of grasping the boundaries of the actual event, assigning a proper
meaning to it, and being the condition for the possibility of its actual
existence. It is as if the brutal event never happened and never left a
visible meaning for the victim, although we know that on the level of
passive spontaneous syntheses it did leave a profound trace.

To use another example, in a study on female victims in Hawaii,
Ruch and Chandler (1979), Ruch (1983), and Luo (1987) remarked

that the victims struggled to bring meaning to the rape experience in order to overcome the sense of helplessness, shame, embarrassment, and concern about family and/or others' reactions opened up by the spontaneous irruption of the intimate space within their lives. As reported by Tsun-Yin Luo (2000), one woman (DR15) raped by her boyfriend initially felt resentment at the rape incident. She indicated that she perceived the incident as premarital sex and she realized later that her perception arose because she meant to preserve the integrity of her intimate life-world; in this way the rape experience never took the meaning of actual violence and even the title "rape" came to be replaced with "premarital sex." One college woman (DR15) raped by her boyfriend chose to continue the relationship because she felt that continuing to see him would "make it [the forced sex] less like rape," and she could stop blaming herself as well as stop feeling sorry for herself. Her psychological defense mechanism failed in its mission; the passive syntheses of her spontaneous life were calling for a meaning that was not fully satisfied by the one assigned by her active intention (Tsun-Yin Luo, 2000, 581–97).

When it is difficult to connect with our own space of intimacy that is forced open by spontaneous passive syntheses, we might witness a low rate of reporting the crime because victims are not willing to recognize the violation of the right to consent as they are not still ready to name that space of consent, even on the transcendental and reflective layer. Additionally, that difficulty shows a lowered level of intimacy of the victim with her/his own self; for this reason, often battered partners and rape victims are more vulnerable with the narratives that burgeon around the event—they can be easily accused of "asking for," "deserving," or "enjoying" their victimization because they are left no intimate space to recollect themselves and the pieces of their meanings.

In the cases reported in this article, the women who are raped by boyfriends, dates, lovers, ex-lovers, husbands, relatives, and other men that they know might represent the tip of an iceberg which reveals a more extensive pattern relating intimacy to forced sexual relations.[7]

From what emerged it seems to be confirmed that due to the spontaneous syntheses which constitute this layer, intimacy is a space disclosed independently of our active, reflective consent. By consent I mean the reflective act of taking responsibility for the already-present passive matter of our lived-experiences and owning it. It may be that sometimes we arrive at this kind of consent, only later through the transcendental reflective layer of intimacy and its active work of meaning-giving activity (*Sinngebung*) while we are doing simple activities such as watching a movie or reading a book. Indeed, on its spontaneous layer when the space of intimacy is forcefully opened the victim is not always immediately capable to recognize the violence because of the already persisting space of intersubjective intimacy and because of the habitual tension to keep that space intact and safe by attributing to it an habitual meaning (which unfortunately is sometimes disruptive to the previous balance and reveals itself to not be fully fitting to the new space). In fact, the former intersubjective space would not accept an immediate change of meanings, and the latter habitual one would resist the destruction brought forth by the sudden change of events. Yet, it may be that the transcendental layer of intimacy can be newly triggered by another spontaneous act of intimacy, which would encourage the victim to repossess her space by giving a proper meaning and a more truthful interpretation to it; this event is what we might call an epiphany. We can see this dynamic in the following story:

> Almost 14 years ago, my first husband attempted to rape me. At the time, we were very close to being separated, and I think he wanted to attempt to bring us closer, back together through a sexual act—he always maintained that that was his prime means of communication, how he felt the closest. At first I fought and when he attempted to smother me with a pillow, I panicked and became only concerned with how to get him to stop—I was afraid he was going to kill me. So I became totally unresponsive to him—wouldn't talk or anything and he eventually stopped tearing my clothes and pulling me and there was no intercourse. Because it happened in the context of a whole lot of bad things in our marriage (he had been violent to me once or twice before, but not sexually so), I didn't have any particular feelings at the time except relief that it was over. Very shortly thereafter, I left him. I never thought of the incident as attempted rape until almost 10 years later when I was walking away from a session of a women's group I was in wherein we had been talking about specific rape incidents that had occurred to some of the members. Until that time, I think I felt rape was of the stereotypic type of the stranger leaping out of the bushes and never thought of an incident like that occurring between people who knew each other, especially husband and wife, as rape. I think this is true of many married women—they have accepted society's dictum that

a man has sexual access to his wife whenever he wants, whether she does or not. Thus, it never occurs to them that this could be a crime, a felonious assault, that this is, indeed, rape.

(Lafree, Reskin, and Visher, Jurors' Responses to Victims'
Behavior and Legal Issues in Sexual Assault Trials,
Social Problems Vol. 32, No. 4 (Apr., 1985), 389–407)

As this interesting interview reveals, the transcendental dimension of the intimate space can be recovered through unexpected awakenings triggered by the interplay of spontaneous passive syntheses and transcendental reflective activity; the new passive syntheses can irritate the lower layers of the spirit and awake it to a new now, from which it can direct its meaning-making activity in a new and more adequate way. That awakening marks the beginning of a process of meaning-discovery that allows for healing that otherwise would be at best incomplete; in fact in order to recover from an experience of forced negative intimacy one should be able to establish a connection with the basic layers of the new intimacy. In cases of violence this reconnection is rarely established because the victim tends to deny the event at worst, or at best to assign a meaning to it that is not fully respondent to the event. The next section will consider the moral freedom that is required to explore the contents of transcendental intimacy.

Morality and Sexual Plasticity

Plastic sexuality is a term used by Giddens (1992) to describe a heightened self-awareness of the fluidity of one's sexual life. Today sexuality has almost completely lost its primary reproductive function; we have sex because we seek pleasure, and the sense of pleasure generally is heightened by self-realization and intimacy. As Giddens remarks,

> When the new connections between sexuality and intimacy were formed sexuality became much more completely separated from procreation than before. Sexuality became doubly constituted as a medium of self-realization and as a prime means, as well as an expression, of intimacy.
>
> *(1992, 164)*

Sexuality is our space of realization because, as Sartre wrote, in that space our facticity is saved by means of the other's regard. In the intimate space of a sexual relationship, whether it is a deep or a shallow relationship, a meaning is given to our facticity, in this case merely to our body, through which we can actually safeguard the meaning of our sexual identity.

The strength of this recognition is proportional to our moral freedom; morality, in fact, limits the space of absolute freedom from which intimacy is generated spontaneously. It is because of moral judgments that victims of rape encounter enormous difficulties in recollecting the actual meaning of their experience. Sexuality needs to be free from moral judgments, for it has a plastic structure that stems from the lower passive layer that is in spontaneous dialogue with our factual existence; in Gendlin's story cited above the moral issue would be represented by the sense of jealousy felt by the wife, and in Zapien's study by the uneasiness experienced by the partners in acknowledging the existing affair. If we allow the first layer to show itself without any moral judgment, we have more opportunity for closeness and recognition with oneself and others. As Moore (1998) wrote, morality is a matter of imagination and courage. If women had never tried to explore new archetypes, the sexual relationship between men and women would have remained in the Victorian era. The sexual revolution allowed the exploration of new territories that now are morally accepted but were inconceivable at that time. Women gained more intimacy with themselves by acknowledging their moral freedom; the sexual revolution opened the doors to a true participative, recursive, and teleological social construction. Although the meanings this construction can bear are potentially infinite, I think that today women are closer than ever before to what they feel is right for themselves.

I partially agree with Giddens when he says,

> Intimacy implies a wholesale democratising of the interpersonal domain, in a manner fully compatible with democracy in the public sphere. There are further implications as well. The transformation of intimacy might be a subversive influence upon modern institutions as a whole. For a social world in which emotional fulfillment replaced the maximising of economic growth would be very different from that which we know at present.
>
> *(1992, 3)*

I agree with the idea that intimacy stems from and exercises a subversive influence on modern institutions; however, it does not represent a democratic institution, but rather a state of nature. The teleological and recursive structure of what we are, is originated from a passive spontaneous layer that rubs against us and calls us to make decisions about the meanings we want to attribute to the former spontaneous experience; at this level we can actively decide whether we want to be intimate with ourselves and choose authentic meanings that define our existence. Hence, more than a democracy, this subversive state reminds me of a state of nature in which we are called to decide if we want to enter a space of co-independence, the so-called civil society. In the space of spontaneous intimacy there is no democratic rule yet; it is on its second layer, that of active recollection and distanced dialogue with our feelings, that we can consider case by case whether the moral laws shared in that democratic co-independence can be more or less meaningful for our sexual existence.

Even the imperative of intimacy—"You have to be intimate! You have to disclose yourself more, not shut people out of your life"—is not a moral rule that can be held in mind in the layer of transcendental intimacy. As Lasch (1977) and Bauman (1990) argued, in matters of intimacy and sexual identity any dependency on experts for self-direction, self-creativity, and unmediated social interaction can constitute a negative influence. Bauman (1991, 205) refers to Sennett's (1977) concept of destructive *Gemeinschaft* in asserting that damage to social cohesion results from the psychological burdens of incitements to mutual disclosure. Intimacy cannot be a moral imperative.

Intimacy is a transcendental space over which we have no control because it opens spontaneously from the depths of our passive life; it represents our facticity talking to us through its teleological and recursive unfolding. The existential exploration that we can undertake of our intimate life is morally free because is meaning-oriented. It represents an active choice to cope with our identity in relation to ourselves and others.

To understand and explore intimacy we need to have a critical distance, be available to break any pregiven moral construction, and participate in the unfolding of its telos. Intimacy is the voice of our core being talking to us and prompting us to make authentic choices; intimacy is not a narrative obligation but a sort of dance with a passive alterity.

Conclusion

In this chapter I showed how sexuality defines our existence when it involves an active choice. This choice, though, being involved in a recursive teleological structure, cannot always be conscious because our factual being is usually a mystery to us, a truth whose essence speaks to us from a transcendental space. Metaphorically speaking, I named this voice intimacy. From the depth of our passive life the meanings that define us and constitute the condition of possibility for our existence come from intimacy, whose structure can be broken down in two main layers—a spontaneous and transcendental one. In our lives we are constantly called on to choose whether we want to pay attention to the constitution of meanings that are going to shape the social category through which we will be recognized. In particular when we encounter cases of forced intimacy that has a negative impact on our psychological balance. If this transcendental voice remains on the layer of passivity, it is likely that our sexual existence will be foreign and meaningless to us; if we manage to attend to this voice on an active and transcendental layer and participate in the constitution of meaning, our sexual identity will be an existential one: the fruit of a choice. Our sexual identity needs to be plastic in the sense that its telos cannot be placed in one category once and for all. To fit in an existential sexuality that is meaningful for us, we need to be free from moral and social constraints and be available to entertain an honest dialogue with our facticity.

Notes

1 *Intimacy* comes from the Latin superlative *intimus* (the most inside possible).
2 I use the word *event* here in Badiou's terms.
3 We are in fact always talking about the volitional body, which makes decisions despite the low level of cognitive awareness involved.
4 Amir's research (1971) on patterns of victimization revealed that 48 percent of the rape victims knew the offender. Forced intimacy arises spontaneously in a place where an intimate space is already created; this generates the problem of naming the forcefulness of the event because the victim desires to keep the intimate space intact. Pauline Bart's (1975) examination of 1,070 questionnaires filled out by victims of rape found that 5 per cent of the women were raped by relatives, 0.4 percent by husbands, 1 percent by lovers, and 3 percent by ex-lovers. Thus, a total of 9.4 percent of the women were raped by men with whom they had intimate relations. Bart's survey also found that 12 percent of rape victims were raped by dates and 23 percent were raped by acquaintances. Less than half of the victims (41 percent) were raped by total strangers. Additional research on rape also reveals a pattern where victims were likely to know the offender or be related to the offender. Of the 250 victims of rape studied by the Center for Rape Concern at Philadelphia General Hospital, 58 percent of the rape victims under the age of 18 were assaulted by a relative or acquaintance. When the victim is a child,

she is likely to be sexually attacked by her father—6 of the 13 children were raped by their fathers (Peters, 1976).

5 South Dakota became the only state to eliminate spousal exclusion from the statute on rape. The 1975 Rape Law reads: "Rape is an act of sexual penetration accomplished by any person...." Other states, such as Florida, do not specifically except married persons from rape prosecution (Silverman, D. (1976). "Sexual Harassment: Working Women's Dilemma." *Quest: A Feminist Quarterly,* vol. 10).

6 Brownmiller, S. (1975). *Against our Will,* Simon and Shuster; Gallen, R. T. (1967). *Wives Legal Rights,* New York: Dell; Griffin, S. (1971). *The All-American Crime,* Rampants, 26–35; New York Radical Feminists (1974). *Rape, the First Sourcebook for Women,* New York: New American Library; Bernard, M. L., and Bernard, T. L. (1983). "Violent Intimacy: The Family as a Model for Love Relationships." *Family Relations,* vol. 32, 283–286; Straus, M. (1980). "Victims and Aggressors in Marital Violence." *American Behavioral Scientist,* vol. 23, no. 5, 681–704.

7   If the perpetrator is known to the victim, people are reluctant to label what transpired as rape. In a study of jurors' attitudes, prior association between the victim and the defendant which would make identification more credible had the opposite result of disposing the jurors more favorably toward the defendant.

(Lafree, Reskin, and Visher , 1985)

Bibliography

Amir, M. (1971). *Patterns of Forcible Rape.* Urbana, IL: University of Chicago Press.

Anderson, W. T. (1990). *Reality Isn't What it Used to Be.* New York: Harper & Row.

Bart, P. B. (1975). "Rape Doesn't End With a Kiss." *Viva,* June, no. 39–42, 100–102.

Bauman, Z. (1990). *Paradoxes of Assimilation.* New Brunswick, NJ: Transaction.

Bauman, Z. (1991). *Modernity and Ambivalence.* Ithaca, NY: Cornell University Press.

Benítez Reyes, F. (1982). *Paraíso Manuscrito.* Sevilla: Calle del Aire.

Cooper, B. (2001). "Constructivism in Social Work." *British Journal of Social Work,* vol. 31, 721–738.

Devitt, M. (1991). *Realism and Truth* (2nd edn.). Englewood Cliffs, NJ: Prentice Hall.

Drummond, J. J. (2003). *Historical Dictionary of Husserl's Philosophy.* Lanham, MD: Scarecrow Press.

Dummet, M. (1991). *The Logical Basis of Metaphysics.* Cambridge, MA: Harvard University Press.

Edie, J. M. (1965). "Transcendental Phenomenology and Existentialism," in *Phenomenology,* (ed. Kockelmans, J. J.). New York: Doubleday.

Foucault, M. (1984). *History of Sexuality, Vol. 1,* (trans. Hurley, R.). New York: Random House.

García, A. (1980). *La Noche Junto al Álbum.* Madrid: Hyperion.

García Montero, L. (2001). *Poemas.* Madrid: Visor.

Gebser, J. (2011). *Ursprung und Gegenwart. Zweiter Teil: Die Manifestationen der aperspektivischen Welt.* Flensburg Fjord: Novalis Verlag.

Gendlin, E. T. (1982). *Focusing.* New York: Bantam.

Giddens, A. (1992). *The Transformation of Intimacy.* Stanford, CA: Stanford University Press.

Henkel, M. (1995). "Professional Competence and Higher Education," in *Learning and Teaching in Social Work,* (eds. Yelloly, M. and Henkel, M.). London: Jessica Kingsley Publications.

Howard, G. S. (1985). "Can Research in the Human Sciences Become More Relevant to Practice?" *Journal of Counseling and Development,* vol. 63, 539–544.

Husserl, E. (2001). *Analyses Concerning Passive and Active Syntheses.* Dordrecht: Kluwer Academic Publishers.

Kelly, G. A. (1955). *The Psychology of Personal Constructs.* New York: Norton.

Koestenbaum, P. (1974). *Existential Sexuality.* Englewood Cliffs, NJ: Prentice Hall.

Lafree, G. D., Reskin, B., and Visher, C. A. (1985). "Jurors' Responses to Victims' Behavior and Legal Issues in Sexual Assault Trials." Social Problems, vol. 32, no. 4, 389–407.

Lasch, C. (1977). *Haven in a Heartless World: The Family Besieged.* New York: Basic Books.

Luo, T. Y. (1987). "Ethnic Variations in Sexual Victimization: A Preliminary Analysis of Caucasians, Asians, and Mixed-Asian Victims in Hawaii," (unpublished Master's thesis). Department of Sociology: University of Hawaii-Manoa.

Luo, T. (2000). "'Marrying My Rapist?!': The Cultural Trauma Among Chinese Rape Survivors." *Gender and Society,* vol. 14, no. 4, 581–597.

Mahoney, M. J. (1988). "Constructive Metatheory: I. Basic Features and Historical Foundations." *International Journal of Personal Construct Psychology,* vol. 1, no. 1, 1–35.

McDowell, J. (1996). *Mind and World.* Cambridge, MA: Harvard University Press.

Merleau-Ponty, M. (1962). *Phenomenology of Perception.* London: Routledge.

Moore, T. (1998). *Dark Eros.* Thompson, CT: Spring Publications.

Peters, J. J. (1976). "Children Who Are Victims of Sexual Assault and the Psychology of Offenders." *American Journal of Psychotherapy,* vol. 30, 398–421.

Putnam, H. (1981). *Reason, Truth, and History.* Cambridge, MA: Cambridge University Press.

Rorty, R. (1991). *Objectivity, Relativism, and Truth. Vol. 1 of Philosophical Papers.* Cambridge, MA: Cambridge University Press.

Ruch, L. O. (1983). "Sexual Assault Trauma and Trauma Change." *Women and Health*, vol. 8, no. 4, 5–21.

Ruch, L. O. and Chandler, S. M. (1979). "Ethnicity and Rape Impact: The Responses of Women from Different Ethnic Backgrounds to Rape and to Rape Treatment Services in Hawaii." *Social Process in Hawaii*, vol. 27, 52–67.

Sartre, J.-P. (1956). *Being and Nothingness*, (trans. Hazel, E.). New York: Washington Square Press.

Searle, J. (1995). *The Construction of Social Reality*. New York: Free Press.

Sennett, R. (1977). *The Fall of Public Man*. Cambridge, MA: Cambridge University Press.

Spiegelberg, H. (1956). "Husserl's and Peirce's Phenomenologies: Coincidence or Interaction." *Philosophy and Phenomenological Research*, vol. 17, no. 2, 164–185.

Stieb, J. (2006). "Rorty on Realism and Constructivism." *Metaphilosophy*, vol. 36, no. 3, 272–294.

Vygotsky, L. (1927). "The Historical Meaning of the Crisis in Psychology: A Methodological Investigation," in *The Collected Works of Vygotsky*. New York: Plenum Press.

Warren, B. (1998). *Philosophical Dimensions of Personal Construct Psychology*. London: Routledge.

Zapien, N. (2017). "The Beginning of an Extra-marital Affair: A Descriptive Phenomenological Study and Clinical Implications." *Journal of Phenomenological Philosophy*, vol. 47, no. 2, 134–155.

6

JEALOUSY

Introduction

First scenario: Kelly and her boyfriend are walking hand in hand on the street, when a very good-looking girl walks by them. Kelly's boyfriend enjoys the view; his gaze lingers—Kelly noticed. Needless to say, their harmony is broken; Kelly and her boyfriend are not walking hand in hand anymore.

Second scenario: a group of friends is having a beer at night in a bar. For most of the night Bob holds the group's attention—everyone keeps laughing at his jokes. Two of the people in the group silently resent the attention that Bob gets with his jokes.

Third scenario: Tina, a young woman, is waiting at the hairdresser for her turn to get her hair done. While distractingly reading a tabloid, she reads a story describing her favorite movie star's extramarital affair. Tina feels bad about it.

Fourth and final scenario: God forbids idolatry because it means rejection of the Godhead as One and Supreme; hence God warns the Israelites[1]:

> You shall not bow down to them or worship them; For I the Lord thy God am a jealous God, visiting the iniquity of the fathers upon the children unto the third and fourth generation of them that hate me.
>
> *(Deuteronomy 5:9)*

The list of these different scenarios can potentially be infinite. What is in common between them? One word: jealousy—or at least what I believe jealousy is. The situations in which this fleeting feeling shows up are innumerable, and it is famously difficult to tame the eruption of jealousy, much less to define it.

What is jealousy? Is it a feeling or an instinct? Looking at these four scenarios we may ask: Does jealousy have anything to do with intimacy? Does it involve love? We often speak of being "jealous of" someone; but does jealousy even require the presence of another person?

In this chapter I will offer an Husserlian grid to interpret the phenomenon of jealousy and provide a description of the layers that constitute this lived-experience. The chapter is divided into two parts: in the first part I will engage with stances that draw upon philosophical positions which I will prove to be different from mine and I will use a clinical case to illustrate my interpretive choices throughout the chapter.[2] Then, in the second section I will use Husserl's phenomenology in order to understand whether jealousy can be considered a feeling, an instinct, or a sentiment and I will employ Husserl's theory of intentionality and his notion of volitional body in order to explain the pre-personal and personal layers of this lived-experience.

I hope to prove that jealousy cannot be put in only one of the above-mentioned categories. In fact, I argue that jealousy is the name of a lived-experience that involves personal and pre-personal layers. On the pre-personal level jealousy is almost an organic affection, like hunger or sleep, which does not involve the presence of a beloved one. On the personal level jealousy is a moral choice about intimacy.

Some Images of Jealousy

A night of dusk, lashing rain and thunderclouds—this is the way in which Strindberg depicts jealousy. All those who ever experienced jealous rage know that this image can be fitting; yet if Strindberg's images work, Toohey (2014, 5) rightfully asks, what makes this dark storm of anxiety, anger, fear different from other states of mind?

A beautiful quote illustrating the variety of states of mind that inform the jealous storm is poignantly worded by Roland in *A Lover's Discourse*, in which he writes, "As a jealous man, I suffer four times over: because I am jealous, because I blame myself for being so, because I fear that my jealousy will wound the other, because I allow myself to be subjected to banality." In this statement jealousy equates to shame, blame, fear, lack of self-confidence; it represents a state of mind that encases one in an endlessly shameful loop.

Ellis was optimistic in saying that civilized people will move beyond jealousy in the years to become. But history proves that we are still there. Why?

Philosophers like Alain Badiou defined jealousy as "a fake parasite that feeds on love" (2012, 59). Solomon thought that jealousy involves "vindictiveness or indignation," both of which entail "moral claims, and not just sense of loss" (1980, 103). Against this claim of Solomon, Wrenn (1989) presents the case of babies feeling genuinely jealous of their mothers, although they do not yet have the developmental tools to feel anything that can be defined as moral. Wrenn then discusses Neu's (1980) definition of jealousy, according to which jealousy equates to the fear of loss. Despite the fact that we might easily agree with this definition, Tov-Ruach (1980) counters Neu's argument, using an example that fits the third scenario I presented in the introduction: "one can be jealous of a distant person: an adolescent might be jealous of a rock star's attentions to a movie star. One needs not be in a real relation to feel jealousy" (103). With reason Wrenn (1989) cites situations in which people feel jealous even if no sense of possession in relation to another person can properly be claimed; moreover, sometimes in feeling jealous *there is actually no other person involved* (as in the second and third scenario presented in my introduction). So according to Wrenn, jealousy is not about loss, but is more about anger and insecurity.

Wrenn's definition brings us back to the question with which we started: why should jealousy be different from other states of mind? Instinctively we know that jealousy is something different from fear, but why?

To this question Wrenn offers a useful answer: jealousy is a three-layered process which involves a conative, cognitive, and affective state which are inseparable from each other. In the last section of the chapter I will return to this structure and discuss it from a phenomenological point of view.

A Clinical Case on Jealousy

Clinical psychology seems to answer the question about the structure of jealousy in a more systematic manner than philosophy. Jealousy, when viewed as psychopathological, is named Othello's Syndrome by clinical psychology (Miller, Kummerow and Mgutshini, 2010) and is a state that occurs in three possible psychopathological scenarios. First, in people with borderline personality disorder, jealousy would present itself as a consuming fear of the partner's unfaithfulness and insincerity. Second, for those afflicted by obsessive-compulsive personality disorder, jealousy manifests itself as a form of ongoing, obsessive, circular thinking that elicits anxiety and fear. Finally, pathological jealousy can "color" disorders that are located in the schizophrenic spectrum; in this case jealousy would be a delusional[3] state in which the person is not fully in touch with what is really happening. This case study from the DSM-IV offers a clear example of the third kind of pathological jealousy (Easton, Shackelford and Schipper, 2008, 264–75).

> Mrs. K is a 39-year-old woman who was brought to the inpatient psychiatric unit by police after being arrested for trespassing on Mr. L's property. Upon arrival, Mrs. K was adamant about being released, stating that she was simply entering her husband's home, adamantly declaring that Mr. L was her husband. She elaborated a story about how much the two of them loved each other, when they got married, and how she was currently pregnant with his child. In actuality, Mr. L used to be Mrs. K's boss, and had fired her because of her inappropriate romantic advances several years prior. Mrs. K was married to another man in Florida, with whom she denied any relationship, stating that she was kidnapped for 4 years, and after escaping, had come to California to be with her husband, Mr. L. Mrs. K was diagnosed with delusional disorder, erotomaniac type, and was started on risperidone.

In this citation jealousy is understood as a pathological state in which the person's feelings are not a response to what is actually occurring. In this case the problem is not limited to the experience of jealousy itself, but concerns mostly the delusional state in which the person lives. From a clinical point of view, as Crichton (2008) remarked, not even Othello would be actually affected by Othello's Syndrome because Othello was genuinely in touch with the reality of his situation, since Desdemona was genuinely attempting to deceive him. His rage was not delusional, since it had a foundation in the actual state of affairs he was experiencing.

Thus, the philosophical positions mentioned above seem to unanimously dismiss jealousy as a disruptive state of mind and to limit jealousy to a specific state of mind. On the other hand, clinical psychology more systematically considers jealousy not a problem in itself, but an affective tone that might "color," in a way that is more or less incisive, a wide range of pathologies.

I think that using Husserl's notions of intentionality and volitional body can unify and harmonize these philosophical and psychological perspectives, bringing together an analysis of the dynamic and affective tone, which belongs to the lived-experience of jealousy.

Practical Intentionality: The Crossroads

As mentioned in Chapter 2, now that Husserl's writings have been almost completely published in the volumes of Husserliana, it is becoming more and more evident that his theory of intentionality cannot be limited to what he wrote in his *Logical Investigations* and *Ideas*. In general, intentionality indicates a *tendere ad* (stretching out toward) that marks out any consciousness' act directed toward its object; it indicates what attends to the existence of the object not within a natural flow of activities, but rather through a reflective aiming at them. Husserl's characterization of intention in *Ideas I* (1913) does not differ significantly from *Logical Investigations*. In *Ideas* intention is described as "seizing upon (…), objectifying turn, <for example> being turned valuingly to a thing involves (…) a seizing upon the mere thing; not the mere thing but rather the valuable thing" (Hua III, 66). Similarly to the *Logical Investigations*, what makes intention an intention in the *Ideas* is the reflective attitude through which we objectify what appears to us. Intention indicates the ability of consciousness to transform undifferentiated matter into a unit of meaning. In the lines just cited from *Ideas*, the practical seizing of sensuous data is explained through valuing activity.

Finally, in the *Anaylses* (2001/1859–1938) Husserl describes intention in the following terms:

> Intention is (…) a presenting endeavor that wants to realize itself in the continuous acquisition of knowledge, in a fulfilling grasp of the self that is constantly in the process of determining more closely, that is, not just in a mere grasping of the self in general, but rather being interfused, with an endeavor into the moments of the object and to see to what extent they are not yet intuitively realized as grasping the self, in order to bring them to this realization.
>
> *(Hua XL, 85)*

In the *Analyses Concerning Passive and Syntheses* (1920–26), Husserl refers to a wide range of intentionalities such as feeling intentionality, affective, intentionality, passive intentionality, instinct intentionality, and so forth.[4] Differently from the general notion of intentionality they involve an affective quality, that we might call tension, with which consciousness attends to the flow of life.

In *Husserl's Ethics and Practical Intentionality* (Ferrarello, 2016) I organize these forms of intentionalities in a system that I argue is the foundation for Husserl's approach to ethical science. This system is a particularly useful grid with which to construe psychological phenomena, jealousy included.

In my reading of Husserl's theory of intentionalities (Ferrarello, 2016) I distinguish at least three categories of intentionalities: active, passive,[5] and practical intentionality. While active intentionality entails a position-taking (*Stellungnahme*) and a meaning-giving (*Sinngebung*) activity similar to what we encountered in Husserl's *Ideas*, passive intentionality is a synthetic process that takes place primarily on two egoless layers, a spontaneous and a non-spontaneous one. These layers constitute the material core around which the meaning-giving activity of active intentionality revolves. The transition from the egoless synthetic process to the egoic meaning-giving (*Sinngebung*) process occurs by means of a practical intentional act. In fact, what Husserl terms the sphere of irritability (Hua, 33, text 1)—that is, the layer of affections and reactions—represents the lowest level of affections from which the ego emerges, reacting to the irritating affecting matter by deciding what position the ego is going to take (Hua, 33, text 1, 5, 6, 9, 10). The ego's reactive emergence stems from the volitional body which bridges together nature and spirit, (*verbindende Bruecke*, Hua-Mat IV, 186); the volitional body bridges nature and spirit through validations because it transforms the willings, drives, and instincts that operate on a passive level into practical actions which affect the organic matter of the agent in a meaningful way. The validations are decided by an ego that responds to the matter by deciding whether or not to accept and validate that matter as its own. Some material contents provided to the ego will remain in the form of egoless passive syntheses; other contents will be recognized and assigned a precise meaning.

We can use the first scenario as an example of the intentional cross-road that takes place within the limits of the volitional body: Kelly leaves her boyfriend's hand not because there is any active intention to show him that she felt jealous, but just because spontaneously she felt unease in walking hand in hand with him. Had he asked her, "why are you leaving my hand?," then she would have been forced to understand what her volitional body decided to do with that feeling whether to acknowledge its meaning in an active intention, by saying "I saw you looking at another girl, I felt jealous," or she might decide to ignore that dynamic and not to say anything, because her body might not recognize it as important or might have solved that feeling in the simple reaction of leaving her boyfriend's hand. Validations have the power to transform what is passively felt into actual actions that will organically shape us; only later will meanings be assigned to those decisions and transformations.

It can happen that the contents of my lived-experience would remain passive, which means that my volitional body would not validate them and no active intention would be triggered into any precise meaning. Kelly, for example, might even not notice that she left her boyfriend's hand. For the passive layers to be determined one needs the intervention of practical intentionality, which represents the "aha moment" in which the ego awakes in its body and takes responsibility for what it lived up to that point. This means that on some level Kelly will always make a choice, whether it is a passive or an active one, although she might not be capable to recognize that choice and interpret the passive courants that informed it.

Hence, within the realm of activity a given number of synthetic layers are constituted in a graspable meaning. The practical intention is a phrenetic act through which the subject decides to move toward a self-constituting act in an act of recognizing the interconnection between passive syntheses and the ego's own activity. If active intention was not interwoven with synthetic matter, every meaning would seem empty and pointless. The bridge between the two is represented by the practical intention, the "*Ich will und Ich tue*" (I want and I do) which operates by means of the volitional body in order to awaken the ego to its present matter (Hua-Mat 9, 128–129, 133). The volitional body is the very first answer that the natural, inanimate thing articulates in response to the there-ness implied by the presence of the physical body. Indeed, the volitional body is a layer constituted by the synthetic activity of apperception and pairing that the ego performs once it awakes from the state of passivity. For Husserl this body as a "living organ of the subject" or an "underground of spiritual life" (2002, 122) is an instrument of perceptions (56) and bearer of sensations (183) which animate the physical body and make it an "aesthesiological body" (284) that can function in the active life. The Body meant as *Fungierende Leiblichkeit* (functioning corporeality) (Husserl, 1989, section 50) mediates between the realm of hyletic syntheses or sub-personality and the world of animate things that are there for us (Donohoe, 2004). The body functions in the world according to sedimented motivations or previous affections that are not yet egoic and originate in the hyletic or natural body. The hyletic or passive material core gives the ego its openness, which allows the ego to constitute its personal layers. (Donohoe, 2004, 64). To use again Kelly's example, the passive layers of her organic body lead her to make an "underground" choice that was not commanded it yet by her ego, but mostly by her organic body.

In the previous chapter I have defined the space between the passive syntheses and the just-awoken I as the space of intimacy, or even existential intimacy. It is on this intimate level that the primal bond between the confused organic life of the body and the meaningful life of the ego establishes a first bond. I consider this bond to be extremely important, because phenomenologically it is only when the volitional body connects properly to the passive life of the body and its active egoic position-taking that life becomes meaningful and grounded in the real world. Kelly can choose to be intimate with her body and give a meaning to her choice, if, of course, she considers that act meaningful.

On the other hand, it can happen that a person cannot establish any connection with the passive layers of the body. In the case of Mrs. K cited in the previous section, it is clear that this condition of connectedness is not yet fully established; hence there is a lack of intimacy in the body-mind of the patient (I will return to this point in the conclusion of this chapter).

In what follows I will use Husserl's notion of intentionality and volitional body as a grid to interpret the lived-experience of jealousy from its egoless arising of passive syntheses to the active egoic position.

Phenomenological Definition of Feelings, Emotions, and Moods

As I will prove in this and the following sections, my position diverges from Neu's, Tov-Ruach's and Badiou's in that I do not think that jealousy can be encased in only one negative category. Rather, jealousy can be a way for our body to point to a direction of greater intimacy and understanding. In that sense, my position is closer to Wrenn's; in fact, I argue that jealousy is a multilayered phenomenon that can be observed on different levels according to what the observer is presently experiencing in relation to her volitional body. I maintain that jealousy will be limited to an instinctual mode if it is allowed to remain on the level of passive syntheses; alternatively, it can become a meaning and even a value if one's volitional body validates the feeling, and egoic activity thereby assigns a meaning to it. In the case of Mrs. K's jealousy for example, jealousy became an existential value and affective tonality through which she interpreted her decisions in an unfortunately delusional direction.

Hence in what follows I will offer phenomenological definitions of the passive space of intimacy made of instincts, feelings, emotions, moods, and motivations, and explain how they relate to jealousy and Husserl's theory of intentionalities.

Thus far I have used the ambiguous expression "state of mind" in order to name jealousy, but this circumlocution does not exhaust the sense of jealousy. Can we consider jealousy an emotion?

According to Husserl emotions are specific forms of feeling-acts.[6] Since emotions belong to the larger category of feeling-acts, they are comprised of an affective and a presentational moment. The affective moment is the most primitive layer belonging to practical and passive intentions. The affective moment represents, in fact, the arising of material reactions that flow from egoless matter toward an egoic structure. On the other hand, the presentational moment is a second, non-spontaneous layer fused with active intentionality; in this moment the ego takes a position that shapes the confused mass of the passive egoless syntheses into a graspable form. The intentional act underlying this latter moment is what Husserl calls an *objectifying act*; that is, a form of directedness of active intentionality through which passive matter is made present to us as an object correlated to an egoic act. For example, when we experience a twinge of jealousy, the experience arises first as a pre-personal experience that is not yet referred to a subject who is experiencing the sensation. Then by means of the underlying presentation, the experience attaches to an object—a valuation or value apperception (*Wertnehmung*) of the arising content matter—and is, metaphorically speaking, colored by affective aspects of the object or state of affairs intended in that emotional experience.[7] This description of the affective and presentational layer of emotions entails that any emotion necessarily contains within it a moment that presents the object with certain descriptive properties. In the second scenario in the introduction to this chapter, for example, the person spontaneously experiences a twinge of jealousy, but it is through the affective and presentational layer that he can understand that this twinge is related to Bob. On a more refined level he can understand that that twinge means that he is not liking Bob because he holds all the attention and if he goes deeper in reflecting on that twinge, he might realize that he does not like that because he feels left behind.

Therefore, what is the object of that twinge and what are its properties? To answer we need to look at the components of the affection; it is in fact through the passive synthesis affectant-affected that any material content is made present to us in a feeling or in the form of an intentional object.

This form of passive synthesis is triggered by instincts and moods (*Stimmungen*)[8] (Hua XXXXII, 262). For Husserl moods exist on a higher level than instincts; they are a synthetic unity of affections that open an affective horizon of possible egoic experiences, experiences which maybe affective, cognitive, or both. Insofar as moods provide an affective context, they do not provide specific intentional direction to an object in the way that feeling-acts and emotions do. Moods instead belong to the layers of passive egoless syntheses. The mood "colors" the experience of objects without revealing its particular affective tonality. Pleasure or fear, for example, are feelings that openly disclose the tonality of a particular experience which we call pleasant or dangerous. Moods, instead, do not belong to the thing itself (Hua XXXXII, 267) but to the arising subjective tonality that colors the apprehension of a lived-experience. On their lower level, moods are what inform the affective moment of an emotion and they connect the sheer affection with egoless matter by stimulating its passivity; on a higher level they translate the passive layers into a turning toward the affecting object. As the original stimulation of passive layers, the affective content of moods stimulates the associative processes of passive synthesis (*Analyses*, section 50) and colors the experience with subjective affective tonalities that are not as fully disclosed as the tonalities of specific feelings or emotions.

On a lower affective level than moods we find instincts: moods and feelings are set in motion by instincts, and they can become part of our habitual emotional life if repeatedly accepted by the volitional body, reinforced by its habits, and interpreted by the same meanings. In the case of Mrs. K the instinct of jealousy certainly became important, habitual, and meaningful because it was reinforced by the actions and decisions made by her volitional body and the interpretations given by her active intentions. In her case, the problem was due to the fact that she was not capable to interpret properly all the passive courants of her organic and emotional life. On instincts Husserl writes:

> The word "instinct" is used in an unusually broad sense, first of all for each drive-intentionality [*Triebintention*], which originally is not yet disclosed in its sense. Instincts in the usual sense relate to remote, originally hidden goals, in a chain of partial drives aiming at these goals and serving the preservation of the species, or, as the case may be, the self-preservation of the individual of the species.
>
> *(Ms E III 10, 6a)*

In that sense for Husserl instinct represents our deeper connection to the hidden goals that regulate our survival. It does not have a content itself; as its etymology shows, instinct refers to an inciting (*stinguere*) into (into); it describes a sudden movement toward something. Instincts and drives set in motion our body through egoless passive syntheses which provide affective contents that feed feelings, emotions, and active meanings. As mentioned above instinct intentionality cannot be equated with the active intentionality that Husserl describes in his *Logical Investigations* because it does not have the quality of referring-to. For example, in the second scenario, feeling threatened by the attention that a friend holds in a group is clearly not the same as going to that friend and telling him to stop. Yet, that feeling has a meaning that is not less important than the sole instinct he felt tingling his attention. Instincts can strongly impact our actions and acquire meanings, but the conscious act of meaning-giving takes place on another level. Hence, drives are intentional because they are part of that force that moves matter to sensuous and categorical syntheses (the two-layered form of passive syntheses), namely to a form that is graspable, but they are not intentional in an active way because they do not involve any representation. Instincts and drives provide the material for the content of the affections that can be expressed on higher level in emotions, or on a lower one in moods. Husserl also wrote that there is a:

> Unity of the process of filling of intention, and this itself is the telos, namely, that the instinctive intention which in a unified way from the start heads towards this interpenetration of intentionality and its releasement and is fulfilled as something unified not in a single phase but in an ongoing achievement (Tun).
> *(C 16 IV, 14, cit. in Lee, 1993, 109)*

The instinctive intention triggers a process of ongoing achievement for which the telos (goal) that moves the reaction between affectant and affected stimulates a chain of passive syntheses, which can ultimately irritate and then awaken the ego's volitional body. Instincts have the strength to move upward from the depth of our organic life to the activity of our decisions. The arc that they describe is what we call *motivations*, which I will describe in detail in the next section.

Motivations, Habits, and Personality

Instincts can become habits when the same instinct emerging in the same given point in time (being hungry at noon, feeling jealous every time my partner pays attention to a person more attractive than I) drives us to the same kind of validation and meaning-giving activity during a period of time (this strange feeling in my stomach means that I am hungry. Hence, I decide that I am going to eat; or, it means that my partner is doing something wrong to me. Hence, I will tell her that I'm feeling jealous). Husserl wrote:

> The personal Ego constitutes itself not only as a person determined by *drives* (...) but *also as a higher, autonomous, freely acting* Ego, in particular one guided by *rational motives* (...). Habits are necessarily formed, just as much with regard to originally instinctive behavior (...) as with regard to free behavior. To yield to a drive establishes the drive to yield: habitually. Likewise, to let oneself be determined by a value-motive and to resist a drive establishes a tendency (a "drive") to let oneself be determined once again by such a value-motive (...) and to resist these drives.
>
> *(Hua IV, 255; En. tr. 267)*

Motivations, which are organic and volitional drives, push the just-awoken ego to take a position in relation to a specific instinct, and validate it according to a specific value-meaning. The repetition of these decisions will shape the personality, behaviors, and even bodily posture of an individual through time.[9] If I allow myself to be overcome by fear, for example, I will tend to assume a bodily posture in which my shoulders hunched inward; my character will be easy to be exaggeratedly impacted by sudden events; and my responses behaviors too will be stilted when threatened by external emergencies. What pervades my active motivation, my egological motivation of one position-taking through another in which my "I" is wakefully involved, is a tug of strivings and willings which take place independently of my I (or *agens intellectus*) on a passive associative level. At this level passive syntheses moved by instincts and drives are the most effective motives, even if the volitional body of my ego might not attend to them; it is at this level, though, that instincts operate as the most basic motives for meaningful habitual constitutions (see: Hua XI, 178 and Lee, 55). Husserl wrote:

> I am not only an actual but I am also a habitual ego, and habituality signifies a certain egoic possibility, an "I can" or "I could", or "I would have been able to", and this ability become actual when it refers to ego-actualities, to actual ego-experiences, that is, as

actualization of ability. In a word, I am (and without this would not be an I, I can not think of myself otherwise), an ego of capacities.

(Hua XIV, 378)

As Husserl recognizes, I am not only the habitual I who awakens in a given moment in time; I am also a stranger who awakens in a body that has yet to be fully discovered. In a life there are momentous awakenings, like falling in love, surviving a near-death experience or potentially fatal disease and so forth, that can push me to a discovery of new aspects of myself. These moments can lead me to retrace the directionality of my lower and higher motivations and can lead me to the constitution of new habits, and accordingly new meanings and values. On the one hand, "good habits" could serve to actualize our ability and allow us to come into existence by fulfilling our qualities and fine-tuning our capabilities. On the other hand habits often limit our ability to creatively explore the multiple directions in which our drives could take us.

The first intimate bond[10] we create then is with our primary alterity, with our I that emerges as a You from the whole of instincts and drives—that is, a bond between our reflective "I" and the pre-reflective, reflexive, ongoing upsurging of our affective and bodily passive life. In the case of Mrs. K this primary bond does not seem to be successfully established, because her interpretation of reality remained in sharp contrast with the interpretation given by the intersubjective community that shared her same reality; hence it seemed that on a certain level there was a missing connection with her intimate organic world. Such a bond is embodied in a sense of "being at home in our own skin," a fundamental comfort with an intimate sense of our own passive life. If this intimate bond is experienced as sustainable in the face of life's challenges, then our decisions will be able to handle and explore the number of passive syntheses that impinge upon ourselves. In this way we can participate in the flow of life as persons capable of adequately reading our felt and bodily sense of life and to attaching to this ongoing flow values and meanings that are consistent to those organic felt senses. Husserl wrote:

> As feeling is founded in the hyletic or the affective tonality [Gefühlsmässigen] of the hyle so the conative as response-form of the I is founded in the affective tonal.
>
> *(E III 9, 16b)*

Ultimately, our feelings, and as sub-categories our emotions, moods, and affections in general, are founded upon the matter, or more specifically upon the syntheses generated by the reactions between affected and affectant. It is from the answer we decide to give to this voice that our personality will be shaped and expressed through behaviors that are more or less consistent with what we actually feel in a given moment. Naturally, what we feel will be always challenged by intersubjective validations. In the case of Mrs. K she was experiencing a form of reality which was fully in conflict with the kind of reality experienced by the people with which she was interacting. Intersubjective validation, which will be further discussed in the next two chapters, is the key to accessing to the realm of normality, the standpoint from which we measure whether or not what we experience belongs to a sphere of normality, abnormality, or hypernormality (see Steinbock, 2007, 28).

Hence, we can say that there is a sort of ascending arc that leads from instincts, drives, affections to moods, emotions, lower and higher feelings. What surfaces and is repeatedly validated by the volitional body becomes established and sedimented as a habit; what remains undetermined can habitually affect our moods, although it will not acquire a specific meaning or value. It is very likely that Mrs. K's issue was not related to jealousy; but her habitual reflex was to validate the twirl of drives and assign them the meaning of jealousy despite the complexity of meanings that those organic layers might have involved. While higher feelings, along with willings and desires, entail an active participation of the ego which determines the affective content of the syntheses in a graspable object, the lower feeling along with emotions, moods, and drives are ongoingly passive and connected to the material life of our body. Lower and higher *motivations*—literally from Latin *motus* (Latin: movement)—are those movements flowing from the lowest level of our organic body (drives, instincts) and connecting lower with higher feelings.

Jealousy and the Vortex of Feelings

What is jealousy then? Though Husserl locates jealousy in the realm of instincts,[11] this does not imply that we need to understand jealousy as limited exclusively to that level. In agreement with Wrenn's (1989) layered interpretation of jealousy, I think as well that jealousy is to be considered as a layered psychological phenomenon. From my point of view this phenomenon involves organic bodily instincts, lower and higher feelings, habits and finally cognitive interpretations. Similarly to fear, hate, and other instincts it is very difficult to name distinctly the instinct. Since instincts are by themselves a form of excitement that pushes a person toward a specific direction, the peculiar essence of an instinct such as jealousy is defined by the direction that that drive tends to assume within the range of actions that a person's volitional body decides to undertake. These actions can be later on interpreted as motivated by insecurity about ourselves, fear of loss, anxiety about a potential change and many other states that the social environment would consider as motivated by the instinct of jealousy—yet the last word about that interpretation is only to the person who is experiencing it. That interpretation only can open a true space of intimacy. As stated above the instinct of jealousy not necessarily reaches the level of meaning-giving activity; while in other cases, it could even be defined as a core value, inseparable—for example—from one's affection for one's partner, or God's relationship to his chosen people. The point is that we cannot foresee what kind of interpretation a person would give to that instinct, but yet giving interpretations marks out the space of intimacy that a person decides to open with herself. A jealous person might have a strong intimate bond with her passive and practical life; she might "decide" to be actively jealous—meaning that she transforms her instinctive jealousy into a motivation, meaning, or values—it might be because her connection to her instinctive part is not filtered by lower and higher feelings and the volitional body decides to validate these instincts. For example, a person might decide to accept the overwhelming input of instincts and validate them through meanings; in that case she might explain her instinctive jealousy as a way of caring for her family and her partner. Conversely, it might happen that a person is seen by the society as jealous but she does not consider herself as such because the interpretation she gives of her passive life is much more refined and precise, in that case the intimate bond established with herself is strong and authentic.

In Othello's Syndrome, for example, the problem experienced by the patient has little to do with actual jealousy, because it relates instead to a factual inability to make a moral choice about intimacy and accordingly to give a consistent meaning to what the person is living. In that case the connection and communication between passive syntheses, volitional body, and active meaning-giving is abrupt and inconsistent and leads to a delusional state (Miller et al., 2010). The active ego was giving voice to a volitional body whose contact with passive syntheses was problematic. The body whose will validates the layers of passive syntheses is not always capable to recognize these layers and accordingly assign them with the right meanings. In fact, in the clinical case mentioned above it is possible that either the emerging I was not able to establish an intimate contact with its passive matter and felt ungrounded in relation to it; or, the emerging I might have experienced contact with its syntheses but was incapable of giving these syntheses an interpretation which was intersubjectively acceptable as meaningful. The woman affected by Othello's Syndrome seems to have been in contact with her passive syntheses—that is, with the organic and affective life of her body—but her interpretation of them was considered delusional from the viewpoint of the person involved in her sense of reality (the others in her life).

Hence, jealousy is primitively a drive, an organic instinct; when it is directed, as any instinct in general, toward a form of self-preservation, the individual might feel drawn to defend the status quo in which she feels safe. Of course, safety is a problematic and very intimate term; we do not, in fact, know what safety means for the person involved—even the homicidal instinct can be considered as defensive mechanism. Therefore we need close observations of the active and interpretative layers of the person's life in order to come to a full understanding of the phenomenon of jealousy as lived by him or her. Depending upon the traumatic events to which one's personality has been exposed during her life, her habitual responses to that instinct of preserving a safe life may be sedimented on a lower or higher level, becoming a full-fledged meaning, a value, a feeling, a mood, or instead just an affection. If a person feels generally safe (with all the meanings that the word can imply), she would not feel driven to thematize her instincts and accept them as meanings or values; rather, they might remain on the level of moods.

For example, in the fourth scenario I presented in the introduction, jealousy is a value, incarnated in the jealous God. In the shared culture of southern Italy jealousy can easily acquire an axiological and meaningful quality because the tendency toward jealousy is seen as conducive to keeping one's family together and avoiding temptation. In the first scenario, jealousy is just a mood that can influence one's bodily reactions, like dropping one's partner's hand, but it is not fully acknowledged by the person who experiences it. In the second scenario, jealousy is a feeling that the person might acknowledge without giving it too much weight. In the third scenario, jealousy is an instinct that might reveal a split between the active and passive layers of the person involved; in this and in the former case, no beloved needs to be involved for that person to feel jealous.

Hence, the instinct of jealousy, which we might call a primordial instinct of self-preservation in response to a threat, can remain locked on an instinctive level or can be gradually validated and emerge on a volitional, axiological and cognitive level either as a rejected or as an accepted instinct. One of the most common ways to summarize these layers is the sentence: "Yes, I'm jealous. You should be happy about it, because this means I care about you."; this might be read from the interlocutor's point of view as "I have this instinct. This instinct might produce a feeling of joy for you and can acquire a meaning of care for me." Of course, this sentence summarizes one version of reality that can be taken either as delusional (in the sense explained above as communicative of an un-understandable concern) or confirmed by the person's partner. This is also the reason why I used four random scenarios in my introduction; the factual instances of jealousy are always very personal and connected to the intersubjective world of the person who is experiencing this phenomenon.

Many people might experience jealousy, and their body might react to that instinct, but they would never decide to acknowledge themselves as being jealous because their rationality (i.e., the validations of their volitional body) will not allow for those underlying affections to acquire a full-fledged meaning. The volitional body of others, instead, is completely pray to this state of mind and feel thrown in its obsessive loop. In both cases the emerging I that owns the volitional body has to make a choice in relation to its affective passive life, and this choice informs the habits, hence the traits, that will shape the person's character.

In the former case, the bodily reactions to affections, moods and feelings of jealousy might still be observable, but the person would never acknowledge them as a genuine jealous reaction because these affections have no meaning for them or conversely have more refined meanings than that of simply jealousy. These feelings are just organic syntheses comparable to being hungry at noon because "I always eat lunch at noon," but then choosing not to eat because "I don't have time to stop until I finish class at 1."

On the other hand, in case the active ego decides to validate the instinct of jealousy and assign a meaning to it, feeling hungry is an important and meaningful signal that one wants to listen to, because otherwise a stomachache or other worse symptoms could occur.

Unfortunately, since jealousy is an instinct first, any meaning or value can provide a fulfilling answer that placates the jealous storm. That is why when jealousy reaches a cognitive level it generates obsessive thoughts; nothing or anything can fully fit in the interpretation of that organic instinct. For example, when our instinct relates to hunger, we can placate the instinct by eating. Conversely, when our instinct relates to something organically more complex like emotional self-preservation, any action we can undertake would be only momentarily placating our anxiety, similarly to compulsive eating. Any meaning or value we can attach to that instinct might feel only provisionally satisfying, because our way to self-preserving our volitional body is complex and built on many different layers.

Conclusion

To answer the questions I raised at the beginning of the chapter: What is jealousy? Is it really a feeling or is it an instinct? Does jealousy have anything to do with intimacy? Does it involve love? Does jealousy require the presence of another person?

We can say that jealousy is rooted in egoless syntheses that assemble themselves on a pre-personal level; this means that jealousy is not properly about love or about an intimate relationship with another person because it arises first at a pre-personal level and it has to do with the space of intimacy that the emerging ego decides to establish with its volitional body. This means that jealousy does not necessarily involve the presence of another person, because it starts as an instinct (like many other instincts, this is the reason why Thooney found it difficult to distinguish jealousy from other states like fear or anxiety) and its most convincing meaning remains always tied to the instinct itself. This instinct is pre-personal and pre-egoic because it is fully attached to our organic matter and calls upon that primordial life in which we are not fully ourselves yet, but we move toward a specific direction. That direction would be a hint to clarify the meaning of that instinct. In this state the emerging ego might interpret that instinct as jealousy, but like any interpretation of organic matter, its meaning can be further refined depending on the level of intimacy and closeness that that person entertains with his or her own body.

To return to the simple example of hunger: when we are hungry, we look for food and we interpret that organic signal with a specific need for food for which we are feeling hungry. Things become much more complex if our body changes, for example with a pregnancy; at that point it becomes more challenging to understand exactly what our body is demanding from us. The situation might become even more challenging if the mother suffers from an eating disorder; in that case her volitional body might be heavily affected by moral judgments with which she weighs her choices in relation to the food that she needs. In this case the dialogue with her body is more problematic and simultaneously less intimate because of the moral barrier set forth by the volitional body.

The same happens with jealousy: our instinct of jealousy may increase or decrease along with the changes our body undergoes or along with the societal and individual's acceptance of that instinct. If we maintain a good level of ongoing intimacy in relation to our volitional body, reasonably free from moral judgments, we might risk discovering what we are actually feeling and give a proper name to it. Differently, if we judge and suppress the volitions of our body without listening to them, it would be easier to fall prey to it and feel increasingly unsafe and dissatisfied.

So, is jealousy, this organic feeling, actual? I think it is. It would be unfair to deny everyone the actuality of what they are living; the delusional, pathological status of what the person diagnosed with Othello's Syndrome is experiencing does not indicate that the person is not actually going through a period of genuine distress; the problem arises on the active level in which the person tries to give meanings to what she is living. In this case the organic signals which affect the volitional body of the subject are interpreted by them in a way that cannot be intersubjectively validated in relation to a community of others; this does not mean that the experience is not actual for the person who is living it. Thus jealousy, especially when disruptive or delusional, comes from one's difficulty in finding an intersubjectively valid[12] interpretation with which to grasp one's affective tonalities.

This is the reason why it is difficult for me to share Havelock's optimism about jealousy. This emotion, like many others—rage for example—has deep roots in human's limited ability to access and communicate with the streaming life of their own bodies and gain awareness of the meanings borne by their bodies. Hence the future of jealousy is up to us, as individuals and as an intersubjective community, to decide how we want to work with the ocean of passive syntheses that inform our individual and intersubjective lives. What is called for, in order to live through eruptions of jealousy more authentically, is commitment to a twofold structure of intimacy: a valuing of and attending to the arising of meaning in the ongoing passive and active layers of our bodies, and an accompanying valuing and attending to meanings in the community of Others with whom we are interconnected.

Notes

1 Of course here I am using one of the many interpretations available for this biblical verse.
2 The decision to distinguish the two disciplines stands here more as a criterion for me to organize the discussion, rather than an actual position I take in relation to their boundaries; in fact as I hope it will become apparent from the rest of the book, I consider these two as being on a theoretical and practical continuum.

3 Here I use the word delusion in the same way as D. Cooper and R. D. Laing did, in order to indicate an ultimate un-understandable attempt to communicate worries and concerns especially in an environment in which this communication was not allowed.

4 I am referring to for example, instinctive intentionality, vertical, longitudinal (Hua XXX), collective (Hua XIV), intersubjective, social, affective, (cf., e.g., Hua XIV, 196ff. and Husserl 1923), vitally flowing intentionality (lebendig strömende Intentionalität) (Hua VI, 259), intentional will (*Willensintention* or *Willensmeinung*) (Hua XXVIII, XXXVII).

5 On the distinction between passive and active Steinbock identified five different meanings: First, A *"lawful, fundamental regularity"* that occurs both actively and passively. Passive terms Husserl uses (as identified by Steinbock) include: "passive genesis," "primordial genesis," "primordial constitution," and "pre-constitution." His uses incorporate both noetic and noematic perspectives. The noetic side involves the "constitution and identity of an object, as well as the forms of connection, coexistence and succession" by the perceptions linger and fade "linking up with previous retentions, motivating pretentions or futurally directed intentions." The noemetic side deals with concordant and disconcordant or harmonious or disharmonious appearances or connections. In this section he also addresses the issue of evidence using the terms "confirmation" and "verification." The former a synthetic function that occurs passively ratifying experience as concordant, while the latter occurs on the active level and "requires various levels of cognitive interventions." (xxxviii–xxxix)

Second, "[A] sphere of the experience in which *the 'ego' is not active, i.e., does not creatively participate or actively orient itself* in the constitution of sense" (xxxix). "This does not mean that no ego is present, but only that the ego is not engaged in active participation" (xl). This leads to a term "active passivity" an activity that does not proceed from action of the ego (xl).

Third, Passivity suggests a realm of bodily habits that were once actively acquired but subsequently have become *sedimented* into a style of comportment, and yet our accessible pre-reflectively (xli). Fourth, Involves the sphere of *pre-givenness* and *object-like formations.*

> Something is pre-given insofar as it exercises an affective allure on me without being grasped by me as such, responsively or egoically … [It is something that] exhibits the basic structure of an object (including an object-phase), but is more "elementary" than an object in the full-fledged sense or has yet *not* (yet) exhibited objectivity.… [I]t is not the result of active processes that give it an identity such that it becomes a theme of cognitive interest.
>
> *(xlii)*

Fifth, related to generativity, in that emergence of an activity arises from passivity, making the active stages possible (from Rees, M. "Co-arising of

Matter and Consciousness, Nondual Potential," unpublished notes, cited with permission).

6 According to Drummond, Husserl distinguishes two forms of feelings, one that does not have the mark of active intention yet and relates to the lower level of affections, sensations, instincts and drives, and a higher one that is regarded as having intentional properties. The lower feelings are those sensory affects that do not bear the mark of an active intention; for example, the sensible pain one feels after breaking a bone or when one has a headache or a toothache. The feelings sensations of pain are referred neither to the bone nor the head nor the tooth as an object of awareness. Nor are they referred to what broke the bone or caused the headache or toothache as their object. The pain is referred to the person (including the bodily parts of that person) who experiences it as its subject, rather than its object. While the pain is related to what causes it, this is a real, rather than an intentional, relation. Feelings-acts, on the other hand, which involve feeling-sensations as moments, are intentional; they are referred to something as their object. So, for example, liking and disliking are the liking and disliking of something; joy and sadness are joy and sadness in something, and so forth.

7 Hua XXXXII, 267:

> Wir bauen, ehe wir an das erstzubetrachtende Apriori, das der bloßen Dinge, herangehen, von diesen nicht nur die Prädikate personaler Bedeutsamkeit ab, sondern auch derartige Prädikate wie die wechselnden Gefühl sprädikat e; und zwar meinen wir hier nicht nur die akt iven Wer tungen, das aktive Gefallen oder Missfallen, das aktive Schätzen, Werten als schön, als reizend usw., sondern die ohne jede aktive Beteiligung der erfahrenden Subjekte auftretenden Stimmungscharaktere und ebenso alle Charaktere triebhaften, instinktiven und sonstigen Reizes, den sie üben, und so überhaupt den weiten Bestand von Erfahrungsmomenten, die wir den Dingen selbst nicht zurechnen, obschon diese sich, sei es gelegentlich oder notwendig, in irgendwelchen solchen Momenten in der Erfahrung geben.

8 It is interesting to observe that in German the word for moods, *Stimmung*, is the root of *Bestimmung*, which means determination. The relationship between purely affective and presentational layer is reflected in the German language too. While in English "moods" or "moodiness" are disparaged as an unreliable source of understanding, in German the moods represent an alluring horizon that opens to further determinations.

9 For example, bioenergetic approach to psychology is founded in this observation; see for example, Reich (1993) and Lowen (1970).

10 According to Hart's (2009) interpretation of Husserl's phenomenology the very first bond with a You that grants my I.

11 Hua XXXXII, 384: "Entwicklung des absoluten Sollens: das Familien-Sollen, das nationale, das humane. Die christliche Nächstenliebe. Aber Instinkte der Flucht, Racheinstinkt, Eifersucht etc.?"

12 This explains why Laing, for example, can still claim that family systems might be at the origin of schizophrenic personality. Schizophrenia might be a healthy response to an intersubjetive sick system.

Bibliography

Badiou, A. (2012). *In Praise of Love*. Paris: The New Press.

Crichton, P. (2008). "Did Othello have the Othello's Syndrome?" *Journal of Forensic Psychiatry*, vol. 7, 161–169.

Donohoe, J. (2004). *Husserl on Ethics and Intersubjectivity*. Amherst, NY: Humanity Books.

Drummond, J. J. (2008). *Historical Dictionary of Husserl's Philosophy*. Chicago, Lanham, MD: Scarecrow Press.

Easton, J. A., Shackelford T. K., and Schipper L. D. (2008). "Delusional Disorder–Jealous Type: How Inclusive Are the DSM-IV Diagnostic Criteria?" *Journal of Clinical Psychology*, vol. 64, no. 3, 264–275.

Farrell, D. (1980). "Jealousy," *The Philosophical Review*, vol. 89, no. 4, 527–559.

Ferrarello, S. (2016). *Husserl's Ethics and Practical Intentionality*. New York: Bloomsbury.

Ferrarello, S. (2017). "Existential Intimacy." *Journal of Constructivist Psychology* (forthcoming).

Hart, J. G. (2009). *Who One Is. Book 1. Meontology of the "I": A Transcendental Phenomenology*. Berlin: Springer.

Havelock, E. (1901). *Studies in the Psychology of Sex*. Philadelphia: F. A. Davis.

Husserl, E. (1973). *Experience and Judgment: Investigations in a Genealogy of Logic*, (trans. Churchill, J. and Ameriks, K.). London: Routledge & Kegan.

Husserl, E. (1989). *Ideas Pertaining to a Pure Phenomenology and to a Phenomenological Philosophy, Second Book*, (trans. Rojcewicz, R. and Schuwer, A.). Dordrecht: Kluwer Academic Publishers.

Husserl, E. (2001). *Analyses Concerning Passive and Active Syntheses. Lectures on Transcendental Logic*, (trans. Steinbock, A. J.). Dordrecht: Kluwer Academic Publishers.

Husserl, E. (2002). *Natur und Geist. Vorlesungen Sommersemester 1919*, (ed. Weiler, M.). Dordrecht: Kluwer Academic Publishers.

Husserl, E. (2012). *Einleitung in die Philosophie. Vorlesungen 1916–1919*, (Hua-Mat 9), (ed. Jacobs, H.). Dordrecht: Springer.

Husserl, E. (2014). *Grenzprobleme der Phänomenologie. Analysen des Unbewusstseins und der Instinkte. Metaphysik. Späte Ethik (Texte aus dem Nachlass 1908–1937)*, (Hua XXXXII), (ed. Sowa, R. and Vongehr, T.). New York: Springer.

Lee, N. (1993). *Edmund Husserls Phänomenologie der Instinkte*. Dordrecht: Springer.

Lowen, A. (1970). Pleasure. San Francisco: Bioenergetics Edition.

McDonald, G. W. (1981). "Structural Exchange and Marital Interaction." Journal of Marriage and the Family, vol. 43, 825–839.

Miller, M. A., Kummerow, A. M., and Mgutshini, T. (2010). "Othello Syndrome: Preventing a Tragedy when Treating Patients with Delusional Disorders," in *Journal of Psychosocial Nursing and Mental Health Services*, vol. 48, no. 8, 20–27.

Neu, J. (1980). "Jealous Thoughts," in *Explaining Emotions*, 434–462, (ed. Rorty, A.). Berkeley: University of California Press.

Ricoeur, P. (2004). *A l'Ecole de la Phenomenology*. Paris: Vrin.

Solomon, R. (1980). "Emotions and Choice," in *Explaining Emotions*, 103–126, (ed. Rorty, A.). Berkeley, CA: University of California Press.

Steinbock, A. (2007). *Phenomenology and Mysticism*. Bloomington: Indiana Press.

Toohey, P. (2014). *Jealousy*. New Haven: Yale University Press.

Tov-Ruach, L. (1980). "Jealousy, Attention, and Loss," in *Explaining Emotions*, 465–88, (ed. Rorty, A.). Berkeley, CA: University of California Press.

Wrenn, M. (1989). "Jealousy." *Noûs*, vol. 23, no. 5, 635–652.

7

AGAPE

Introduction

In this chapter I will discuss love in the sense of the Greek *agape*, often translated as love, affection, or charity. In these pages love will be described as a vital affective force, that binds together the layers of our society as a whole. Since this force can be binding and caring, as much as brutal and annihilating,[1] this chapter will unpack and analyze the effects of love within the society understood as an intersubjective whole. The goal is twofold: to understand the constitutive process through which love gathers together society as an intersubjective whole; and to analyze the way in which singular individuals come together in the whole of the society.

For this reason the first part of the chapter will be dedicated to an analysis of pre-predicative and predicative intersubjectivity and will show how time and empathy, in particular the affection of time and the affection of matter, play an important role in the constitution of these layers. The second part will study the notion of normality and how the harmony of love may conflict with the ought of individuals' love and their sense of normality.

Pre-Predicative and Predicative Intersubjectivity[2]

"Subjectivity is intersubjectivity" (Hua XV, 74). Husserl affirms in his manuscripts dedicated to the topic of intersubjectivity. The paradoxical flavor of this sentence can be taken as an invitation to consider intersubjectivity more as the name of a problem rather than an actual solution. In fact, in relation to intersubjectivity one might ask how can a subject live an authentic life if one's life is intersubjective? How is individualism possible if our subjective way of living is intimately intersubjective? How can my sexuality be completely fulfilled within a normal society? How can my love for someone be a unique form of love within the intersubjective social web of normativity?

On the one hand intersubjectivity seems to explain how we communicate with each other, but on the other it seems to be seriously undermining our chance to be our own self. In one of the volumes dedicated to the study of intersubjectivity, Husserl explains the polarity ego-monad and intersubjective subject in these terms. He writes:

> I have to distinguish: the currently transcendentally phenomenologizing subjectivity (as an actual ego-monad) and transcendental subjectivity as such; the latter turns out to be transcendental inter-subjectivity, which includes the transcendentally phenomenologizing subjectivity within itself.
>
> *(Hua XV, 74–75)*

This passage shows that we are individuals exactly in virtue of the polarity between nature-spirit, matter-reflection, pre-predicative and predicative layers. In fact, this polarity is what makes us humans; that is, organic living things and units of sense. Both sides of the polarity are monadic and intersubjective at the same time. The intersubjective component is transcendental[3] because it represents the condition of possibility for me and other subjects to be subjects and a community at the same time. The transcendental subject presents itself primarily not in the form of an ego, but etymologically speaking as a *sub* (beneath)-*iectus* (placed); that is, something that is placed underneath the weight of pre-predicative matter. The monadic phenomenologizing ego is the one that commits itself to reflect upon the pre-predicative matter in order to recover its sense. Yet, as we saw from our previous investigation this reflection is possible because the intersubjective matter awakens the ego from its status quo and pushes it to an affective reaction that generally resolves itself in the acceptance or the refutation of the given matter. It is through this reflection that we, as egoic monads, become aware of the intersubjective web in which we live. As Fink (1981, 66) noticed, the primordial subjectivity of this intersubjective structure arises in the form of a primordial, anonymously functioning center (1988, 74) that yields the continuous awakening of an I which is not yet fully individuated. The ultimate ground of all distinctions is pre-egological and transcendental.

Intercorporeality[4]

It is in this light that we can read another important Husserlian statement, "the we has a collective corporeality" (Hua XXXVIIII, 81, 51). Intersubjectivity is not just an idea or a good intention, but it is primordially actual matter; my flesh is not only mine but is continuously shared with others while it is mine.[5] This entails that the intersubjective web within which subjects exist as individuals and intersubjective bodies is actually incarnated. We are others[6] in the way in which we handle our body and even more primordially, in virtue of the life that we actually receive from our parents.[7] At the same time we are selves because of the choices we make in our daily life as are they coming from a monadic reflecting ego. Hence, Husserl explains the constitution of this corporeal community first[8] from a pre-predicative point of view, through what I called the affection of time; and second from a predicative point of view, through what I called the affection of empathy. In the next section I will describe more in detail what I mean by affection of time and affection of empathy; for now it is important to say that the intermediate step between the two is characterized by the awakening of the ego under the influence of the affection. Indeed, on the pre-predicative level the "we" is an incarnated and intersubjective whole that has not performed yet any active reflection and analogizing pairing (Hua XV); on the predicative level the reflecting activity of the monad is triggered by the ego which awakes under the pressure of pre-predicative affections, such as the affection of time, and a predicative one, such as the affection of empathy. It is through empathy that we discover our relative separateness and autonomy as a unique core with respect to others and it is through time that we are given actual matter upon which we can take actions.

As we saw in previous chapters, the dynamic bond that needs to be established in order for individuals to become self-aware dormant monads within an intersubjective whole is a predicative intimate bond. I connect with myself because I decide to own the matter that is attached to my body; yet, this bond remains quite challenging because whenever I validate my own being and I decide to give a meaning to it, other scattered matter of being remains submerged and escapes my sight. Hence the question, how can one live a veritable and harmonious life with one's own self and within a collective community if even its flesh escapes its grasp?

A way to address the question is by focusing on the transition between the pre-predicative to the predicative layer; what I called elsewhere, practical intentionality. According to Husserl, nature is a unit of identity constituted through an intersubjective mutual understanding (Hua-Mat IV, 215). As he wrote in text 9, (Hua XXXVI) nature can be experienced as a correlate of the harmonious experiences of a community of embodied subjects who are capable of acknowledging each other's existence and the existence of one and the same nature. In Nature[9] we are the *echte Dasein* (exact being); that is a unity coming from associative syntheses. I become myself and at the same time a *Universalitaet der menschlichen Daseinsverflochtenheit* (universality of human interwoven beings) through my volitional body and its *Ich kann* (I can) (Text, 32, Hua-Mat IV, 453); meaning that I discover my material being as I awake from my passive state and decide whether or not to own this passivity. The material being that is attached to my body cannot be considered as monadic because it is built upon my already-given interwovenness with others' experiences, but my responsible decision is.

Hence, in order to understand how the associative syntheses will announce my being within the society, I need to look at the interplay between passive, active, and practical intention. As a part of the hyletic intimate bond that the ego establishes with its own sphere of existence, the intersubjective bond is an ongoing process that can never be concluded. The awoken I that emerges from the layers of passive syntheses opens itself to an horizon that continuously broadens as the formation of sense goes on. As Reyanert remarked (2001, 207–216), in the fifth Cartesian Meditation Husserl showed that the I that awakes from passivity has already objectivated its biological and living body as similar to the biological body of the other. In this recognition (which Merleau-Ponty called the reversibility of the flesh) the body of the other is co-constitutive of the world and more precisely of myself as living in that world. This is why Husserl claims that a phenomenological discussion of subjectivity in the end turns out to be a discussion not simply of the I, but of the *we* (Husserl 1962, 245–246, 1970, 340, 1973c: 74–75, 1999, 30), and this is also the reason why he writes that all truth and all being have its intentional source in transcendental intersubjective sociality (cf. Husserl 1999, 156).

These two layers alone explain why in our sexual intersubjective community if one adopts sexual behaviors that are considered inappropriate by the community, even if those behaviors do not directly affect anyone personally, they nevertheless have the power to offend others. What we are and whatever we do triggers a process of co-constitution of incarnated meanings to which others will to attend, whether one wants it or not.

An example of this interconnection is an awkward political campaign that was launched in Italy in 2016. The claim of this campaign was "fertility is a good that belongs to everyone"—the questionable claim gives immediately the sense for what is meant by intercorporeality. In a very clumsy way the Italian minister of health initiated the campaign with the good intention of encouraging Italians to have more children. The images they chose for the campaign were in my opinion as inappropriate as its claim; they use, in fact, a leaking water spigot with a woman aside holding an hourglass in her hand. The message was clear: "women do not waste a common resource, do not be selfish, your fertility is going to expire soon and does not belong only to you!" Needless to say, a wide range of people who cannot have children for several reasons, felt offended by the kind of species' selfishness manifested in this message.

Clumsiness aside, this campaign might be a good example to show how intercorporeality works on its pre-predicative intersubjective layer. In fact, in this case the intersubjective corporeal whole was moved by the drive to self-preserve the species, which was expressed through an inconsiderate message toward the bodies of the whole. On the pre-predicative level sexuality was treated as an intersubjective common good whose aim was reproduction and on the predicative level as an obligation in which the *Allersubjectivitaet* (all-subjectivity) prevailed over the individual, and thus produced stereotypical meanings.

In this and other cases it might happen, in fact, that the meanings constituted within the community do not match one's own personal validating system and hence individuals might want to try to change them. As Theunissen (1984) remarked, in this intersubjective interplay I experience the Other as experiencing me in an alienating way, and this leads me to ultimately experience myself as a stranger.

On a pre-predicative egoless level, since I am not yet fully aware of what is me, meanings seem to "just happen" to me, and if I let them happen, they might even define me and shape my body. To use the example above, if the social pressure about having a baby is too strong around me, I might passively opt to become pregnant without actually owning this decision. Yet, this decision will actually change my body and my life in a decisive way. As noticed by Zahavi (2014, 54–58), on this level I am not the sole constitutive Other, because my I is everyone (2014, 55) and my body is my body because it can reflect on the body of someone else's that is analogous to mine. It takes an act of practical intention to be able to be a subject and decide how much otherness should be part of my self. My *res extensa* can become mine because I can give it a meaning through the analogizing act which would allow the transition from the pre-predicative to the predicative layer of my being.

My self, I, and finally my body, can come to existence in the world through an horizontal transcendental activity that by nature is constitutively made of others; the Other precedes and enables my very existence as an individual being. As Zahavi wrote, the "Transcendental subject understands itself better as transcendental intersubjectivity" (1997, 63). In fact, my own transcendental I is a transcendental Other with a centering I that comes to a predicative existence through a validating choice which applies on two layers: *Seinsboden* (the ground of being) and *Allersubjectivitaet* (all subjectivity). In the former case we have the ontological foundation for everything objective as a primordial field of interrelated absolute subjects; in the latter case, the *Allersubjectivitaet* has a correlate in the *Zwischenraum* (the interspace) where the transcendental total subjectivity actually dwells as intercorporeal being. Steinbock (1994a) criticized Zahavi's interpretation of this: while for Zahavi the recognition of personal ownership passes through the personal narrative of a psychical ego, for Steinbock this recognition is mid-way between being organic and cognitive—to name it I used practical intentionality and the volitional body. According to Steinbock, whose position I am more sympathetic with than that of Zahavi, the individual and intersubjective person come to existence through a dynamic force whose name is love. It is in fact through an affective pull that human beings come together and decide to take responsibility for their own matter. Affection is the term that Husserl uses to explain the force that guides together these spontaneous passive syntheses; similarly, affection is the force that brings the material being together to a new form, whether this is a person, a family, a society, a group, and so forth.

As discussed in this section, any individual is constitutively an intersubjective and a monadically incarnated whole, which comes into existence through three layers, gathered together by the emotional force of love, and organically expressed in the form of affection. In the next two sections I will explain in detail how this force works on the pre-predicative and predicative levels: the one that belongs to the pre-predicative layer I name the "affection of time," the one that belongs to the predicative level, I call the "affection of empathy."

Intersubjectivity and the Affection of Time

As we saw from Chapters 2 and 3, the constitution of meanings always takes place in the now-moment of awakening in which our volitional body decides to validate the material content presented by sensuous passive syntheses. From there the non-spontaneous categorical syntheses form a now-here that Bergson called "attention a la vie."

In his *Phenomenology of the Social World*, Schutz, referring to Husserl's manuscripts, explains that the constitution of sense in time happens through longitudinal and transversal intentionality. Longitudinal is the intention toward the retentions (toward the flow of consciousness) (1959, 379ff., 82ff./ C, 108ff.); through this form of intention every now captured by the I is a discrete moment (1959, 52) of a primordial activity. These nows represent a quasi-temporal disposition of the phases in the flux of time. Moreover, each now, according to Schutz (1959, 57) is the expression of a reflexive intention that Mohanty names primordial self-presence (Mohanty, 2008). When the I awakes in the moment in time it comes to presence through a primordial functioning that fulfills an immediate goal (2008, 61). There is a reflexive presence in the longitudinal intention through which I come to existence; this presence explicates itself through the validation of my voluntary action (2008, 66). In this now I extend myself toward immediate contents that are going to fulfill the horizon of the now (2008, 63) that I retained as what was prompted to me through action—what Husserl called retention.

It is from this retentive side that the transversal sense of intentionality stems. Schutz describes this form of intentionality as being a constant synthesis of identity (1959, 55). While the transversal intentionality is responsible for the constitution of the same object through its movements and modifications, longitudinal intentionality knits together the moments of sense that constitute that identity (Hua X, 39). We might say that longitudinal intentionality belongs more to passive intentionality, while the transversal intentionality belongs more to practical intentionality.

Transversal intentionality uses re-presentification and rememoration in the synthesis of the same. In fact, re-presentification allows the recollection of the external experience of the world to become present to my reflecting ego. Since this sameness is conveyed to me through moods, bodily feelings, thoughts, etc., its meaning will continuously shift according to the way in which the affects—first of all the affect of time—influence our experience. In fact, the immediate problem that arises from the intersection of transversal and longitudinal intentionality in the constitution of the *Allersubjectivitaet* is the emotional affect of time. The "source-point" (*Quellpunkt*) of the enduring object in the flowing stream of consciousness is the "primal impression," "tone-now" (*Tonjetzt*), that affects my consciousness in a continuously changing now. As this "tone-now" is modified into "something that has been," the primal impression passes over into retention: "the tone-now changes into a tone-having-been; the *impressional* consciousness, constantly flowing, passes over into an ever new *retentional* consciousness" (Hua X, 31). Retention, impression, and protention are smaller fragments of the time-affection that keeps the flow of our consciousness running in the crossroad of longitudinal and transversal intentions; they not only "hold in consciousness what has been produced and stamps on it the character of the 'just-past'" (Hua X, 88)—ensuring that consciousness is always "consciousness *of what has just been* and not merely consciousness of the now-point of the object that appears as enduring" (Hua X, 34)—but each retention is also retention of the elapsed tone retention, including in itself "the entire series of elapsed intentions in the form of a chain of mediate intentions" (Hua X, 123). In this way, retention "extends the now-consciousness" (Hua X, 47) such that the "now-apprehension is, as it were, the head attached to the comet's tail of retentions" (Hua X, 32).

Time is intersubjective at its core; that is, it is one of the primary reasons that subjects are primordially intersubjective. It is through time that we come to be one and many at once and we can create a *Zwischenraum* (interspace) and *Mitwelt* (in between-world) in which we share our existence. A case in point can be the situation in which in a family system, one of the members (the mother, for example) is affected by a disorder that involves a distorted sense of time. In that case the children might flow with her sense of time more easily than her therapist does because the sense that they happen to constitute together comes from a pre-predicative *Zwischenraum* (interspace) whose time texture runs wider and deeper than the one shared with the therapist. As Zahavi remarks, generally it is the interpenetration of drives that lead to the fulfillment of the two streams of common time. Yet, if this interpenetration is not possible the co-presence (1997, 98) of the two kinds of intentions can trigger a coincidence of foreign forms of temporality that influence each other; this interpenetration happens without us fully realizing it. In our family, in a couple, or in our workplace, the way in which we live in and are through time is fully guided by the constitution of one's dominating temporal stream that influences and co-constitutes others' streams. Full individuation can take place through an active effort of reflection on the layers of temporal constitution that affects our body; this individuation would help us to distinguish what is originally mine from what belongs to others.

Affection of Empathy[10]

As I will show in this section, affection of empathy and affection of time are interconnected in the intersubjective constitution of Being. While the former is pre-predicative and material, the latter is predicative and spiritual; the former concerns the way in which the matter organizes itself in nature, the latter entails an actual effort of emotional and cognitive reflection on the Other. The *Leib*, that is the living body, constitutes itself through its kinaestheses; that is, through movements and experiences that are localized on a material level. Indeed, as Chapter 4 demonstrated, what distinguishes the constitution of a living spiritual being from the constitution of a material one, is its movement and the localization of its experience. The body is always a *Mitdabei* (being in between), a "there," a complex of sense organs. As far as we know the two strata cannot exist without each other for human beings; in its first stratum the body is a material thing (*Koerper*) and then, given its ability to move and to perceive, it is the center of orientation, or basic stratum, for the real mind and the givenness of the I to move and live.

Real independent minds originate by means of a two-tiered constitution. On the one hand they connect to the living body (meant as *Natur*), and on the other to the spiritual I that emerges after bracketing the natural attitude of the empirical I (*empirische Ich*) or the human I (*Ich-Mensch*) (Hua IV, sections 20, 27, 49, 57) that is present in the stream of naïve and pre-reflective experience. I experience myself as having a biological body (*Koerper*) – which is the first layer of the mind's constitution; and I experience my body as an animated (*beseelen*) soul or psyche. Therefore, I experience myself as a living body (*Leib*) or animal organism, but I discover myself as not merely a body because I experience myself as having what Husserl terms a spirit (*Geist*) as a member of the social world. We can know the Natural pole of things and their essence only by approximation, since as transcendent objects they are unknown to us. In contrast, we can grasp the other pole of the stream, the spiritual one, as a noema or act-complex comprised of three layers: material thing, living thing, and mind.

While on the first two levels the affective force of time (which as I said before, is one of the main components of love) plays an important role for the constitution of the intersubjective subject, it is on this third

level of constitution that Husserl mentions empathy (*Einfuehlung*) (Hua
IV, sections 43–47) as a key concept by means of which we can explain
the constitution of the living body and its own world.

Husserl's earliest unpublished material on the problem of empathy and
the constitution of the living body dates from 1908 (Hua XIII).[11] There
he presents the problem of empathy in the following way: the temporal
stream of experience that flows through the two poles, Nature and
Spirit, essence and reflection, is absolute, but at the same time it is bound
to my body. The body, as a material thing, is constituted through certain
law-governed interconnections in a continuous chain of protentions and
retentions. Yet, at the same time this thing is my body and the stream to
which its absolute or a "this-there" (Hua XIII, 5) now in time is connected is my stream. Yet, from here a few questions come: How can the
absolute be bound to what is mine? And how is it possible that my body
is different from another person's body in this absolute flow? Husserl's
answer would be: "To go deeper into the question of the other in relation to I, we have to delve deeper into the constitution of the thing"
(Hua XIII, 13). On this point he provides the following arguments (Hua
XIII, 17–20):

1. Everything that is given to me as content of my reflection is repeata-
   ble in my consciousness and in other (human consciousness) as a
   doxic content.
2. Yet every consciousness perceives its own contents, connected with
   the *haecceitas*, the individual real things that are different from each
   other. Any conscious being perceives the contents of its consciousness as comprised of a multiplicity of objects.
3. It is not on the level of real things, perception, essences or on the
   level of the Natural pole that the empathic experience and accordingly the individuation of the ego can take place, but it is on the
   level of pre-empirical temporality or on the level of Ur-experience
   (i.e., on the level of the first constitution of the thing) that I can presentify my body as a stream of "nows" whose moments are fulfilled
   with sensuous data analogous with those of another body.
4. The body is a thing that I feel as constituted within a sensuous synthesis or a proto-experience.

As we saw from these points, time and empathy are interwoven in the
constitution of the layers of human proto-experiences in which we
recognize ourselves as belonging to our absolute flow of time and as
being that absolute flow. In order to understand how transversal and

longitudinal intention of time interacts with empathy, in the next section I will describe two kinds of empathy: a straightforward and an oblique.

Straightforward and Oblique Empathy

In the *Bernau* manuscripts of 1918 and in *Husserliana* XIII (Text 15, 97) Husserl distinguishes between straightforward and oblique forms of empathy—a distinction that recalls the same two trajectories of time, transversal and longitudinal. Oblique empathy is an act analogous to recollection, while straightforward empathy is a form of presentification. Indeed, while in the former kind of empathy I have an experience in which I *presentify* the other's experience, in the latter I *reflect* on the experience of the object and I fulfill the expectation with what I recollect from my past (Hua XIII, 97).

The world emerging from my monadic reflection is first of all solipsistic (my thing, my body, my mind) and it is empathy that opens up windows in this blind monad. The Other is given to me as a present presence, or better, as another presence tied to the here and now of my body (Hua XIII, 99). Here for the first time Husserl tries to extend the reduction to intersubjectivity: "I remain throughout in my field, which through empathy has extended itself to the sphere of a plurality of closed flows of consciousness (called I-consciousness), which are connected with my flow of consciousness through interconnections of motivations of empathy" (Hua XIII, 87; Mohanty's translation, 2008, 100). It is after this reduction that the Other appears primordially as a now with its field of protentions and retentions. In this "now" I find a way of being, a mode, posited as a self-given in which experiences that are not my own are directly present to me. In this sense, following a text of 1910–1911 (Beilage XXVIII; Hua XIII, 229) empathy is a mode of apperception and appresentation that is founded on another concrete apperception (the apperception of the living body or the material thing). It is a *Verbildlichung*; that is, an act of analogizing or picture-making. Empathy presupposes the empathized object as a being that is given in the now. The now is not continuously self-intuited: in the empathic act you do not feel the continuity, because that continuity is pre-temporal and already constituted in the point now. In the empathic act, taken as recollection, the now is mirrored or given by another ego in the constitution of a harmonious spatio-temporal nature. Through the empathic act, taken as recollection, we go beyond our own egoic stream and reach other egos' streams. Empathy constitutes a new form of transcendency

(Hua XIV, 8) because, despite the fact that we do not know of the contents of other persons' streams as first-person experiences, we can interact with them as units constituted in time and recollected in the apprehension.

What emerges in relation to the affection of time and empathy addresses the same questions raised above: how can a subject live an authentic life without crosscurrents of influence from the others? How can we be individuals if our subjective way of living is intimately inter-subjective? Despite Leibniz's monadology, it seems that there is a window in the current of affections in which we have the choice to be aware of who we are and decide how much of ourselves we want to be with others. This answer, though, leaves open the problem of authenticity. Our authentic being is always influenced by and made of the sense of normality dictated by the intersubjective whole, both on a predicative and pre-predicative level. Hence the question, how can we be authentic if our authenticity risks to be labeled as abnormal? This question will be addressed in the next section.

Normality

Husserl's researches on normality and abnormality are collected in the D 13 group of manuscripts entitled *Urkonstitution*, or *Primordial Constitution*.[12] Husserl began to reflect on the notion of normality in *Ideas I* and then he further developed his researches in January 1931 (Hua XIV, text 10). In these texts normality is considered as the answer to the *Weltfrage* (the issue of the world). The world for us is never fixed or rigid. Volume XLII of the Husserliana is dedicated to the case limit or *Grenzsituation* that relates to the relativity of our experience with respect to normality and abnormality. The world is what is constituted in sedimentations of layers of cooperating co-subjects. In this normal constituted world, abnormality represents one of the many possible structures of its layers. In fact, in this sense normality (*Normalität*) represents one of the many possible horizons of familiarity in which the world is given to us (Husserl, 1973a, section 46 and section 93) and through which we expect to experience (*Vorgriff*, *Vorhabe*) new objects. Therefore, we define "normal" as how we expect to live according to an already-constituted intersubjective "style" of life, while "abnormal" refers to what breaks or disrupts any pre-delineated expectation. While normality indicates "concordance" (*Einstimmigkeit*) with regard to certain objects (Husserl, 1973b, section 21), or practical familiarity with expected experiences (Hua IV, section 59), abnormality stands for a lack of certain faculties and capacities to relate to the world in the expected way (Hua I, section 55).

In text 13 of Husserliana XIV Husserl explains how the discovery of me as a normal material thing, then as a normal body, and finally as a normal mind is constituted in time according to a double form of lawfulness: the causality of things and the psychophysical conditions of the mind. The transcendence of the thing differs from the transcendence of the ego due to this system of appearance.

My normal body is in general the presupposition for expected basic and empathic interactions with others mainly performed through movements (text 16, Hua XIV). According to text 17, the original being of my body is a pre-reflective being or a being constituted in an original experience that makes me recognize any other as a co-subject. If an abnormal material thing were to appear to me, it would be recognized by me through an actual communication (Hua XV, text 29); even if the object does not actually talk to me or move toward me, I can penetrate its being through its language or any contact with her body (by *Ontifizierung*). Thus, the transcendent appearance of this object would demonstrate a causal and psychophysical lawfulness.

In this case empathizing with someone I consider abnormal would be classified as normal, because I can present that object (the abnormal person) as actually understandable within my lawful system. The sense-data that I can gather from my interaction with her and my habitual repetition of this interaction might fulfill the act of expectations in the chain of protentions and retentions by virtue of the familiarity that I feel for this body; and if I grouped the sense-data belonging to that person, they would appear analogous to the sense-data belonging to my living body. The two systems of appearances would turn out to be normal, familiar, or harmonic, at least on an individual basis. This means that from my point of view I can empathize with someone who others consider abnormal if I predispose my sense of normality to be expanded by another system in a straightforward and oblique way; that is, if I can appresent the Other as a living person that interacts with my own sphere and I can recollect her data as meeting my outlined expectations.

The problem that will still stand in relation to abnormality is that the intersubjective system might easily decide to not validate the other "abnormal" system in order to maintain consistency within the identity of the already validated intersubjective system.

The Intersubjective Answer to Normality

On the one hand, from an intersubjective perspective an empathic presentation and recollection cannot always be validated as normal; abnormality is an exception that, fortunately, is constitutive of normality. For example, it would require an important empathic and temporal stretch for a family to understand the structure of a masochist if none of the people involved in that intersubjective system have never experienced masochistic drives. It would take the experience of time and feelings before the family would be capable to integrate that appearance into a new psychophysical lawfulness. As Steinbock correctly remarks:

> Normality is essentially an intersubjective notion, not defined in advance, and is the very relation of living beings to their environing world and to other living beings of the same type. As a relational concept, normality is a constitutional notion (...). Normality and abnormality arise through a lived relation with the world and others, and it is from and through our lived human normality or abnormality that we as humans can encounter the normality and abnormality of other species incommensurate with our own.
>
> *(1994a, 569)*

From the perspective of social ethics, empathy, as well as time, are the constituents for intersubjective feelings. As Husserl writes, "we become acquainted with the real and exclusive ethical attitude (...) in the actual ethical will or through living empathy [*Einfühlung*] of such a will." (Hua XXXVII, 246). In this quote Husserl shows how empathy as apprehension (*Aufassung*) and positing (*Setzung*) allows me to apprehend what belongs to me through a positing volition, and what I perceive as mine through others' co-apprehensive perceptions (Hua I, section 44). By virtue of this modification I can decide to endure in that state of modification and renew it throughout all my life, both as individual and as a part of my social community.

Indeed, as a result of this analogical apperception—as Theunissen (1984, 89, 150) rightly reads it—"the ontological foundation of a meaningful society is possible if human beings voluntarily accept and extend themselves in an empathic interconnection with each other, which includes being altered by the co-presence of the others in the validation of abnormality."[13] According to Theunissen the objective I is constituted by alteration (*Veranderung*) and this alteration is patently reified in my body "I become something else." For example, I might need plastic surgery to become closer to the idea I have of myself or I want to read all that my favorite philosopher wrote because I want to interiorize her as much as possible—in these ways "I extend myself toward the Other" be the Other an ideal or an actual being. The objective I is made of the ongoing alteration of its personality and by the ongoing confirmations of the changes that the alteration requires. Both these forms of alteration bring to an assimilation of the alterity that keeps the process of the egoic constitution always open.

The community might not accept altering its identity in the same way as I accept to alter mine because they do not love the person who is altering my identity as much as I do. Yet, the alteration will take place as well on an intersubjective level, although on a smaller scale. To follow up on the example I provided above, it might be that through the affection of empathy and time I find a way to merge with a masochistic person even if my erotic drives do not primordially match with hers; yet this intersubjective synthese might be frowned upon by the larger community because it would involve an alteration of goals that does not seem to lead to any common good.[14] Maybe, this empathic apperception would not be perceived as healthy as expected by the social community because not every personality would reasonably like to be altered according to these drives. Yet, it is also true that in the span of Western civilization for example, it is thanks to those who altered our consideration of children, women, animals, environment, that we had a chance to improve the quality of our life—these categories were normally retained as hardly living. This alteration resulted in a more well-rounded, but not yet perfect consideration of human being and living things. This is to say that we cannot actually tell yet what we will be able to integrate in the future of our society.

As mentioned above, society is conceived of by Husserl as a many-headed subjectivity, founded on the acceptance of individual egos, such as academic associations, professional organizations, to share a community of will (*Willensgemeinshaft*). Maybe in the future we will be willing and able to extend layers of otherness as a constitutive part of us that cannot be conceivable for us today.

> We do not only live next to one another but in one another. We determine one another personally (...) from one I to another I. And our wills do not merely work on Others as the components of our surroundings but in the Others: Our wills extend themselves unto the will of the Other, unto the Other's willing which at the

same time is our willing, so that the deed of the Other can become our deed, even if in a modified manner.

(F I 24, 128 quoted in Hart, 1993, 248)

In this quote Husserl shows in more detail how the interaction with the Other alters and determines us.[15] Our will seems to be the leading force of what we decide to accept as normal or abnormal parts of what eventually is going to constitute us as individuals. Yet, as we can deduce from this passage, a privileging and quasi-sacralizing attitude of collective determination in the service of a higher form of identity could lead to the acceptance of, as in fact happened, a totalitarian political order. I believe that Husserl's high praise for a community of will (Hua III, 108) and love as an eudamonistic bridge to the Other should be always ethically balanced by the personal commitment to individuation through a reflective life.

Community of Love[16] and its Imperative

To come back to the questions raised at the beginning of the chapter, how can the individual's best become a common best within a normed society? How can I be at the same time a part of the community as a whole, and a whole myself? How can my sexuality be completely fulfilled within a normal society? How can I express the uniqueness of my love for someone within the social web of normativity?

The bonding force that seems to bring together the volitional bodies of an intersubjective human community is love, that, in the light of Hart's (2006, 2009a, 2009b) and Drummond's (2015) discussion,[17] might be defined as exceptional. "The law of love reigns" (Husserl, Ms. F I 24, 38a, b) in the lawfulness of a natural order that is continuously co-constituted. From a predicative point of view one's absolute ought is that of empathizing with and being caring toward one's neighbor; the same can be said from a pre-predicative point of view, the scattered matter of one's being seems to come together to form a meaning for me because of this force of affection (we proved this in Chapters 2 and 3). "The values of neighborly love are by far the biggest part of the values of an absolute ought." (Husserl, Ms. F I 24, 38a, b). Text 9 of the second volume *On the Phenomenology of Intersubjectivity* opens with Husserl's description of love as the feeling that ontologically links individuals together as "a spiritualized corporeity" (172, 175); once more, love is presented as a bonding force that connects body and mind, matter and spirit through the pull of affection. (I will explore the corporeal agapic meaning of love in the next chapter.)

Reflecting on this point, Melle (2002, 231) considers love as that which allows a human being to pass through the transition from *animal rationale* (rational animal) to *animal amans* (loving animal), or as we stated above nature and spirit, matter and reflection, pre-predicative and predicative being.

> Love is a value that determines the intersubjective constitution of the individual such that the individual is not just isolated in its monad, but intersubjectively connected to others without losing itself. The lover does not lose herself in love, but lives in a special (...) way as herself (an I) in the beloved, which is beloved individually for her.
>
> *(Ms. F I 24, 29a)*

It is through this ontological value[18] that we can determine the plurality of our desires and drives.

As Melle emphasized, the "community of love" (*Liebesgemeinschaft*) constitutes the highest form of sociality for Husserl because it is through love that people support each other, foster their vocations, and empower their real becoming. Husserl does not indicate any special political form for love's realization. As a value that translates natural lawfulness, according to Schuhmann (1991) love leads to a form of community that overcomes any classical form of political organization. Thus, love should be the *telos*[19] of the community and its categorical imperative.[20]

Love, like any sentiment, can be habitualized, but as a self-reflecting and determining value it can express its sense only when it is actively exerted. Only if I decide to commit to and act upon the awakening that love elicts in my spirit, I can give a meaning to the synthesis with which my self and the others are given to me.

> With the opening of the eyes to the universality of one's own life and the life of the community, the absolute ought and the circle of absolute calls becomes expanded, and finally embraces the whole world of values and the personal world in the unity of one synthesis [...].
>
> *(Husserl, Ms. A V 21, 117b)*

My absolute ought—committing myself to what I really am—means faithfully loving myself as the first Other that I encounter. Husserl talks about the "truth of will" to explain the way in which one's self reveals its absolute ought to itself as an absolute evidence. That "truth" is the very first sense of love (Hua XLVII, 410–420).[21]

Love is the absolute belief in the beloved as the unique Other (e.g., 354, 463–471) and thus it requires trust in my own good will and that of the other. "I must believe necessarily because of being I myself and a member of humanity, and because of my existing in regard to my actual surroundings as a beneficent agent" (Hua XLII, 407).

The ought of love is declined as well in a pre-predicative and predicative layer. Feelings are not motivated by an unconditional form of love that is at work as a vocation or an inner calling, similar to the care that a mother can have for her child.[22] This form of love exists prior to reflection and any predicative activity. In this case the intentional act is not motivated or founded on the affection that is taken and valued by the subject, but as a response to a more primordial call. There is an unconditional "you ought!" followed by a necessary "you must!" that does not depend on a legitimate obligation (*rechtmässige Bindung*). This affection precedes all rational explanation, even where such explanations are possible (Ms. B I 2, 65a quoted in Melle, 2002, 238–239).

Within this interpretative framework Husserl poses the *ought* of love on the inferior spiritual level and its *must* on the superior one. We are called to love as a necessity that is fully grounded in any reason (or reflective presentation) we can provide.

The Ipseity of Agapic Love and its Absoluteness

Coming back to the discussion between Hart and Drummond I referred to at the beginning of the previous section, Hart, differently from Drummond, interprets Husserl's notion of love as exceptional. While for both scholars love is expressed in a mind-body imperative, for Drummond love cannot be personal, but it is in its intrinsic nature agapic since it refers to an original intersubjective being that constitutes our Ipseity (sameness). This Ipseity is close to a primordial substrate for personal properties that does not need any property in order to be since it is absolute and independent. Yet, according to Drummond this substrate is not an independent part, because it is always caught in the co-founding process from which the I draws its identity and self-awareness. My personality is the necessary *accidens* of that substrate that defines it as Ipseity. If I understood Drummond's argument correctly, the substrate mentioned by Hart cannot be the same as the Ipseity, because this latter requires a self-awareness that would be impossible by definition for an absolute substratum. What is absolute cannot be an *Ipse*. At best the Ipse is the *accidens* that always tries to fully grasp that totality. "The Ipseity is an abstraction, not a self. The experiencing agent, the person, is the basic *concretum* for discussion of selfhood" (Drummond, 2015, 58). Love cannot be a characterization of an abstraction, since it is a material drive (as shown in Chapters 2 and 3) that necessarily moves the *concretum* (the agent) to feel something that is founded in this sentiment of necessity.

From my way of reading of Husserl's interpretation of agapic love, it seems that both Drummond and Hart are right; love operates as inter-subjective primordial and pre-predicative substratum that we recognize as a cofounded *concretum* and as a monadic Ipse that is given to us in the form of an absolute. For Hart love is a characterization of Ipseity of personal properties, while for Drummond the Ipseity refers to an absolute. "Love arises from the empathic perception of the Other (...). Love, an intentional act that fulfills the respect burgeoning in empathic perception is directed to 'somebody' a person. One does not love somebody, with no delineated features" (Hart 2009a, 209). Nevertheless, Hart says, "our central thesis is that love's primary intuitional target is another person's Ipseity, that is, the Ipseity as incarnated and personified" (Hart 2009a, 215). The other's personal properties manifest a kind of transparency in relation to the Ipseity that is the general source of the person (Hart, 2009a, 210). Hence, love intends the Other through and beyond her distinguishing attributes (Hart 2009a, 184, 2009b, 282). Drummond objects to that that no kind of love can escape the foundational relationship, and therefore any form of love is absolute.

Yet, from what I gathered in the analysis of this chapter, I believe that love is addressed to the Ipseity and the relational substratum at once because love is a layered feeling that binds togehter primordial and complex layers. Sometimes we love something more primordial than the intrinsic quality of that person, we love her matter, or *concretum*, that speaks to us in a way that we cannot fully understand even after reflection; other times we find confirmation of the instinct of love in the specific qualities that motivate us to love a person.

Drummond explains the process of predicative constitution I proposed above through these four kinds of founding relations:

1. Reciprocal supplementation: the sense B founds sense A that is to say that sense B (color) is supplemented by sense A (shape) to form the complete compound sense C shaped color and vice-versa colored shape.

2. Presupposition: to say that the sense B founds the sense A is to say that sense A (bachelor) presupposes sense B (male).
3. Motivation: to say that sense B founds the experience "&" for a subject S is to say that sense B (the man as armed) intentionally motivates, that is, is a motivating reason for S, to experience & (fear) with its axiological correlate (danger).
4. Justification: to say that the sense B founds the sense A is to say that sense B (the man as armed) provides justifying reasons for sense A (the armed man as dangerous and fearsome), where the justification can be either inferential or non-inferential.

According to Drummond, love in general involves both presuppositional and motivational foundations. Agapic love in particular also involves the fourth form of foundation, justification (Drummond, 2015, 61). This means that, according to him, in the founding relationship love is founded in the *concretum* subjective agent on at least three levels.

Erotic love, for example, is founded on the bodily features of another person. My erotic love for another person cannot be justified, but it can be motivated by the sight of the other's body. On the other hand, familial love is based on respect and is motivated by the care that my parents have for me. In this latter case we encounter a form of agapic love that might be felt as abstract but is motivated by the admiration that we feel for the way in which a person lives; this call cannot be ideal or absolute. I respect and agapically love a person because of the qualities that this person manifests; as Drummond states, "These qualities are a motivation" (2015, 66). It follows that agapic love is both motivational and justifying love (Drummond, 2015, 66) whose absoluteness is grounded in an ongoing relational force. From my point of view, if Drummond's thesis is correct, love is absolute and relational at once, since it always depends on one or more foundational relationships. Second, love would always require a *concretum* or an agent who puts it in practice. This agent, since it is a *concretum*, cannot be an absolute and therefore cannot go beyond—as Hart argued.

Conclusion

This chapter was focused on the study of the intersubjective community as it is constituted on a pre-predicative and predicative level. I explained how love is a bonding force on a pre-predicative (lawful) level and an absolute ought on a predicative (normative) one, and how the two knit together the scattered matter of being. This process of constitution around an organic and spiritual ought is brought together by the affection of time and empathy. These two kinds of affective forces reveal on both levels how the intersubjective whole is constituted as an egoless flow of synthetic matter and a reflecting egoic act of responsibility. The notion of normality emerges from the interplay of these two layers as an egoless validation of the scattered matter of being and the responsible act of owning and giving meaning to what has been validated. As concerns the questions raised above, how does the individual's best can become a common best within a normed society? How can I be at the same time a part within the community as a whole, and a whole myself? The answer lies in our deep understanding of the process of passive constitution of life and our ability and will to assign a meaning to it. From there the other questions—How can my sexuality be completely fulfilled within a normal society? How can I express my love for someone within the social web of normativity? How can a subject live an authentic life without being influenced by others?—can be addressed. In fact, we build normality every day in what we passively constitute within our society and in the way we decide to answer in the call of love according to our predicative mode. The choice of altering the intersubjective community starts on a pre-predicative passive level, but it is on the predicative level that conscious meanings are constituted in the contribution of the collective notion of normality. In that sense, the agapic force of love seems to be the glue that keeps together the scattered matter of our Being around a core of sense that each one of us continuously contributes in building both by means fo aware (predicative) and unaware (pre-predicative) choices.

Notes

1 See for example what Plato wrote about love in *Republic*, book VI.
2 See Hua XV, 74: "Subjectivity is intersubjectivity"

> I have to distinguish: the currently transcendentally phenomenologizing subjectivity (as an actual ego-monad) and transcendental subjectivity as such; the latter turns out to be transcendental interusbjectivity, which includes the transcendentally phenomenologizing subjectivity within itself (Hua XV, 74–75). We now know that Husserl had discussed the aforementioned problem with Pfaender and Daubert already in the summer of 1905. The question which proves to be fundamental from the beginning is that which concerns the "principium individuationis" of the single consciousness. How does it happen that I am the same throughout the transformation of "my" mental acts [*Gefuehle*]? What

does the word "my" signify in this connection? "What is the foundation for this selfness," asks our philosopher. Contingent sensuous material can offer no explanation of this identity and unity. In his investigation—as so often—Husserl proceeds from an analysis of the perceiving consciousness. "The appearances which I have from my standpoint (place of my physical body in space), I cannot have from another standpoint ...,

Husserl states.

3 Merleau-Ponty thus concurred with Fink's main criticism of Kantian philosophy, namely, that it is not genuinely transcendental but rather remains "worldly" [«mondaine»], in that it ultimately takes the world for granted and makes use of it, rather than, as Merleau-Ponty put it, "wondering about the world and conceiving the subject as a transcendence toward it" (PhP viii).

4 Intercorporeality is a term introduced by Husserl, developed by Fink, and commonly known through Merleau-Ponty. (Husserl (PhP xiii, 415; SNS 237/134, 1960, 97, 1964d, 107, 1973, 45).

5 This can be easily proven on a physiological and neuronal level. Intercorporeality contains, at its core, the perception-action loop between the self and the other (Tanaka, 1945/2012). The self's perception of the other's action prompts the same action in the self (e.g., contagious yawning) or a possibility of the same action (e.g., smiling). Thus, it is through our motor capacity that we understand the meanings of other's actions (Kono, 2005). Our basic ability to understand others is perceptual, sensorimotor, and non-conceptual (Gallagher, 2004). Bodily resonance precedes the theory or simulation put forward in the ToM ability. This basic interpretation of intercorporeality corresponds well with the empirical findings on the mirror neuron system, which provides the neural basis for the perception-action resonance between the self and the other (Rizzolatti and Craighero, 2004; Rizzolatti and Sinigaglia, 2008).

> Communication or the understanding of gestures is achieved through the reciprocity between my intentions and the other person's gestures, and between my gestures and the intentions which can be read in the other person's behavior. Everything happens as if the other person's intention inhabited my body, or as if my intentions inhabited his body.
> *(Tanaka, S. The Notion of Intercorporeality and Its Psychology, 102 Bulletin of Liberal Arts Education Center, Tokai University (1945/2012, 190–191))*

Besides the discovery of mirror neurons in the area of neuroscience, after Merleau-Ponty's death in 1961 many empirical cases have been reported in social and developmental psychology that support the notion of intercorporeality. The following cases are considered classical and are well known in the field. *The Notion of Intercorporeality and Its Psychology*, 104 Bulletin of Liberal Arts Education Center, Tokai University; Reflexive crying (Simner, 1971): Newborn infants have a strong tendency to cry in response to another newborn's crying. It is said to be the earliest stage of empathy. Neonate Imitation (Meltzoff and Moore, 1977): Newborn infants imitate an adult's facial expressions, such as opening and closing the mouth or sticking out the tongue. Postural congruence (Scheflen, 1964; LaFrance and Broadbent, 1976): During communication in pairs or in a group, a similarity in participants' postures is often observed (e.g., crossing the legs, head propping, leaning back). This is correlated to ratings of rapport between individuals and involvement in communication (Bernieri and Rosenthal, 1991). Synchrony is based on the rhythmical circulation of action and reaction between self and other. It is important to add that this circulation is based on the embodied perception of each other's action. From an enactive point of view, perception is not a process of passively receiving information from the environment. On the contrary, it is a process of exploring possible action toward the environment, based on embodied skills (Varela et al., 2004).

Fuchs and De Jaegher (2009) describe this as follows:

> When two individuals interact in this way, the coordination of their body movements, utterances, gestures, gazes, etc. can gain such momentum that it overrides the individual intentions, and common sense-making emerges (…). Each of them behaves and experiences differently from how they would do outside of the process, and meaning is co-created in a way not necessarily attributable to either of them.
>
> *(476)*

6 Buddhism and Stoicism, for example, already proved this statement right in the principle according to which harming another is the same as harming oneself since we all belong to the same body.

7 As Fink wrote: "The awakening of an immeasurable wonder over the mysteriousness" (KS 115f/109). This wonder involves the loss of naïve obviousness, the disconcerting astonishment of which "displaces man from the captivation [*Befangenheit*] in everyday, publicly pre-given, traditional and worn-out familiarity with existents." It "drives one from an always already authorized and expressly laid-out interpretation of the sense of the world," with the result that the phenomenologist

> once again opens himself primordially [*uranfänglich*] to the world, finding himself in the dawn of a new day of the world [*in der Morgendämmerung eines neuen Welttages*] in which he, and everything that is, begins to appear in a new light.
>
> *(Fink 1966, 183)*

8 I use numerals, but I invite the reader to keep in mind that in fact the linear order of time is at work in the phenomenological analysis. So there's no actual order, but just a narrative need for me to express this concept. More on this point in the next section.

9 Word that we might read not just as the wild life we come in contact with, but as the primordial locus in which we find ourselves through our awakenings.

10 According to Daly's (2015) reconstruction of intersubjectivity, empathy is the second layer of the intersubjective constitution.

11 Husserl began to reflect on this point in 1905. In a discussion with Daubert and Pfaender (Mohanty, 2008, 278) Husserl wonders, "what is the foundation of the self sameness (*Selbstgkeit*) that I retain admits changes of my experiences?"

12 See for example, manuscript D 13 XII, 12: "Die Normalitaet bezieht sich auf die Spezies."

13 And vice-versa it is the positions of professionals such as physicians, nurses etc—who cannot afford to be modified by the co-presence of the others because they need to be effective. See on this point Daly, 2015.

14 On the notion of teleology, intersubjectivity and normality see: Husserl, Krisis 2, 152, 173, 327, 329.

15 See: Drummond, "Forms of Social Unity: Partnership, Membership and Citizenship" in *Husserl Studies*, 18: 141–156, 2002 and "Political Community" in Thomson, Kevin, and Embree, Lester, eds. 2000. *Phenomenology of the Political*. Dordrecht: Kluwer Academic Publishers.

16 On this point read: U. Melle, "Edmund Husserl, from reason to love" in *Phenomenological Approaches to Moral Philosophy*, J. Drummond and L. Embree (eds), Dordrecht: Kluwer Academic Publishers, 2002; J. Drummond, "Moral Objectivity: Husserl's Sentiments of the Understanding", in *Husserl Studies*, 12, no. 2 (1995), 165–183; J. Drummond, "Exceptional Love", in *Phenomenologica 216*, 2015, 51–69; K. Schuhmann, "Probleme der Husserlschen Wertlehre", in: *Philosophisches Jahrbuch* 98 (1991); 106–113.

17 According to Drummond (2015, 51) the target of love is not propertiless Ipseity of the Other, but the concrete person of the other over time. My love of a particular person is motivated by certain attributes of that person and those attributes vary according to the type of person. Agapic love is not an ideal kind of love. It is a form of love that is motivated and justified by certain kinds of attribute. Drummond uses his view on the intentionality of feeling to prove these three points, arguing "the statement according to which an intentional act has to be a founded act should be reinterpreted noematically" (52, but also Drummond 2002, 2009). I take a number of feelings as the properties x, y, z and these properties noematically found my state of mind. The intentional feeling presents its object as having a particular set of non-axiological properties that I takes as value-attributes (*Wertnehmung*) that motivate the intentional act and its affective response. In turn the a ective answer does or does not justify the valuation accomplished (Drummond 2015: 53). it leads to a rational way of interpreting the intentionality of feeling. Indeed, axiological understanding of real properties justi es the evaluation that motivates the feeling.

18 More on the ontological concreteness of values in my *Ethical Experience*, Bloomsbury, 2018.

19 This good-in-itself, which qualifies Myself in interpersonal loving in this primordial epiphany, is received whether we want it or not and "before" we could subject it to our volition.

20 I do not see a strong discontinuity between the two Husserl ethics 1914 (Hua, XXVIII) and 1928 (Hua, XXXVII]. Just as in his early ethical writing, in Husserl's late work the categorical imperative is still universal and connected to the personality of the individual. In his later ethics it is perhaps easier to see the emphasis Husserl places on the genetic aspect of his ethics and its integration in an intersubjective society. In "From Reason to Love," 242–244, Melle speaks of the early ethics as the "ethics of the categorical imperative" and of the later ethics as the "ethics of renewal" and the "ethics of love." Nevertheless, I think that the categorical imperative is strongly present in Husserl's lectures of 1908, 1914, 1920, and in his articles and notes from 1923 to 1930. Dividing Husserl's ethics in two periods is useful but not necessary. On the one hand the distinction marks more neatly the difference between the "rationalistic" versus the "affective" side of Husserl's early and later ethics; on the other hand the distinction can lead readers to view Husserl's ethics through an unnecessary dichotomy. For further reading on Husserl's later ethics see: Melle, U. (2007) "Husserl's Personalist Ethics", in *Husserl Studies*, 23, no. 1, 1–15; Hart, J. G. (2006) "The Absolute Ought and the Unique Individual," in: *Husserl Studies* 22, no. 1, 223–240; Buckley, P. (1996), "Husserl's Rational 'Liebesgemeinschaft'", in *Research in Phenomenology* 26, 116–129.

21 In Hua XLII, especially Numbers 14 and 30 and Hua XI, 214ff., and 226ff. we find important roles assigned to the heart (*das Gemüt*).

22 Parenthetically, this famous example provided by Husserl represents one of the many cases of social pressure toward the construction of normal agapic categories. In fact, it can certainly happen that a father more than a mother can feel that calling; it can happen as well that women will never feel that call.

Bibliography

Bernieri, F. J. and Rosenthal, R. (1991). "Interpersonal Coordination: Behavior Matching and Interactional Synchrony," in *Studies in Emotion & Social Interaction. Fundamentals of Nonverbal Behavior,* 401–432, (eds. Feldman, R. S. and Rimé, B.). New York: Cambridge University Press.

Buckley, P. (1996). "Husserl's Rational 'Liebesgemeinschaft'", *Research in Phenomenology*, vol. 26, 116–129.

Daly, C. (2010). *An Introduction to Philosophical Methods.* Toronto: Broadview Press.

Daly, A. (2015). *Merleau-Ponty and the Ethics of Intersubjectivity.* London: Palgrave Macmillan.

Drummond, J. (1995). "Moral Objectivity: Husserl's Sentiments of the Understanding." *Husserl Studies*, vol. 12, no. 2, 165–183.

Drummond, J. (2000). "Political Community," in *Phenomenology of the Political*, 29–53, (eds. Thomson, K. and Embree, L.). Dordrecht: Kluwer Academic Publishers.

Drummond, J. (2002). "Complicar las emociones." Areté: Revista de Filosofía, vol. 14, 175–189.

Drummond, J. (2009). "Feelings, emotions, and truly perceiving the valuable." The Modern Schoolman, vol. 86, 363–379.

Drummond, J. (2015). "Forms of Social Unity: Partnership, Membership and Citizenship." Husserl Studies, vol. 18, 141–156.

Drummond, J. (2016). "Exceptional Love." Phenomenologica, vol. 216, 51–69.

Fink, E. (1966). Studien zur Phänomenologie, 1930–1939. The Hague: Martinus Nijhoff.

Fink, E. (1970). "Husserl's Philosophy and Contemporary Criticism," in The Phenomenology of Husserl, 73–147, (ed. Elveton, R. O.). Chicago: Quadrangle.

Fink, E. (1981). "The Problem of the Phenomenology of Edmund Husserl," (trans. Harlan, R. M.), in Apriori and World: European Contributions to Husserlian Phenomenology. The Hague: Martinus Nijhoff.

Fuchs, T. and De Jaegher, H. (2009). "Enactive Intersubjectivity: Participatory Sense-making and Mutual Incorporation." Phenomenology and the Cognitive Sciences, vol. 8, no. 4, 465–486.

Gallagher, S. (2004). "Understanding Interpersonal Problems in Autism." Philosophy, Psychiatry, & Psychology, vol. 11, 199–217.

Hart, J. (1992). Person and the Common Life. Dordrecht: Kluwer Academic Publishers.

Hart, J. G. (2006). "The Absolute Ought and the Unique Individual." Husserl Studies, vol. 22, no. 1, 223–240.

Hart, J. G. (2009a). Who One Is. Book 1: Meontology of the "I": A transcendental phenomenology. Dordrecht: Springer.

Hart, J. G. (2009b). Who One Is: Book 2: Existenz and transcendental phenomenology. Dordrecht: Springer.

Husserl, E. (1962). Phänomenologische Psychologie. Vorlesungen Sommersemester 1925, Husserliana 9, (ed. Biemel, W.). Den Haag: Martinus Nijhoff.

Husserl, E. (1969). Zur Phänomenologie des inneren Zeitbewusstesens (1893–1917), (ed. Boehm, R.). The Hague: Martinus Nijhoff.

Husserl, E. (1970). Crisis of European Sciences and Transcendental Phenomenology, (ed. Carr, D.). Evanston: Northwestern Press.

Husserl, E. (1973a). Zur Phänomenologie der Intersubjektivität. Texte aus dem Nachlass. Erster Teil. 1905–1920, (ed. Kern, I.). The Hague: Martinus Nijhoff.

Husserl, E. (1973b). Zur Phänomenologie der Intersubjektivität. Texte aus dem Nachlass. Zweiter Teil. 1921–28, (ed. Kern, I.). The Hague: Martinus Nijhoff.

Husserl, E. (1973c). Zur Phänomenologie der Intersubjektivität. Texte aus dem Nachlass. Dritter Teil. 1929–35, (ed. Kern, I.). The Hague: Martinus Nijhoff.

Husserl, E. (1989). Cartesian Meditations, (trans. Cairns, D.). Dordrecht: Kluwer Academic Publishers.

Husserl, E. (2001). Natur und Geist: Vorlesungen Sommersemester 1927, (ed. Weiler, M.). Dordrecht: Kluwer Academic Publishers.

Husserl, E. (2002). *Natur und Geist. Vorlesungen Sommersemester 1919*, (ed. Weiler, M.). Dordrecht: Kluwer Academic Publishers.

Husserl, E. (2008). *Die Lebenswelt. Auslegungen der vorgegebenen Welt und ihrer Konstitution. Texte aus dem Nachlass (1916–1937)*, (ed. Sowa, R.). New York: Springer.

Husserl, E. (2014). *Grenzprobleme der Phänomenologie. Analysen des Unbewusstseins und der Instinkte. Metaphysik. Späte Ethik (Texte aus dem Nachlass 1908–1937)*, (ed. Sowa, R. and Vongehr, T.). New York, Springer.

Kono, T. (2005). *The Mind Extended into the Environment*. Tokyo: Keiso Shobo.

LaFrance, M. and Broadbent, M. (1976). „Group Rapport: Posture Sharing as a Nonverbal Indicator." *Group and Organization Studies*, vol. 1, 328–333.

Melle, U. (2002). "Edmund Husserl, from Reason to Love," in *Phenomenological Approaches to Moral Philosophy*, (eds. Drummond, J. and Embree, L.), Dordrecht: Kluwer Academic Publishers.

Melle, U. (2007). "Husserl's Personalist Ethics," *Husserl Studies*, vol. 23, no. 1, 1–15.

Meltzoff, A. N. and Moore, M. K. (1977). "Imitation of Facial and Manual Gestures by Human Neonates." *Science*, vol. 198, 75–78.

Merleau-Ponty, M. (1962). *Phenomenology of Perception*, (trans. Smith, C.). London and New York, Routledge.

Mohanty, J. N. (2008). *The Philosophy of Edmund Husserl, 2 vols*. New Haven: Yale University Press.

Rizzolatti, G. and Sinigaglia, C. (2008). *Mirrors in the Brain*. (trans. Anderson, F.). Oxford: Oxford University Press.

Rizzolatti, G. and Craighero, L. (2004). "The Mirror-neuron System." *Annual Review of Neuroscience*, vol. 27, 169–192.

Scheflen, A. E. (1964). "The Significance of Posture in Communication Systems." *Psychiatry*, vol. 27, 316–331.

Schuhmann, K. (1991). "Probleme der Husserlschen Wertlehre," *Philosophisches Jahrbuch,* vol. 98, 106–113.

Schütz, A. (1959). "Type and Eidos in Husserl's Late Philosophy," *Philosophy and Phenomenological Research*, vol. 20, no. 2, 147–165.

Schütz, A. (1967). *Phenomenology of Social World*. Evanston: Northwestern University.

Simner, M. L. (1971). "Newborn's Response to the Cry of Another Infant." *Developmental Psychology*, vol. 5, 136–150.

Steinbock, A. J. (1994a). "Homelessness and the Homeless Movement: A Clue to the Problem of Intersubjectivity." *Human Studies*, vol. 17, no. 2, 203–223.

Steinbock, A. J. (1994b). "The New 'Crisis' Contribution: A Supplementary Edition of Edmund Husserl's 'Crisis' Texts." *The Review of Metaphysics*, vol. 47, no. 3, 557–558.

Tanaka, S. (1945/2012). "The Notion of Intercorporeality and Its Psychology," *Bulletin of Liberal Arts*, Education Center, Tokai University, vol. 102, 190–191.

Theunissen, M. (1984). *The Other*. Cambridge: MIT Press.

Varela, R. E., Vernberg, E. M., Sanchez-Sosa, J. J., Riveros, A., Mitchell, M., and Mashunkashey, J. (2004). "Anxiety Reporting and Culturally Associated Interpretation Biases and Cognitive Schemas: A Comparison of Mexican, Mexican American, and European American Families." *Journal of Clinical Child and Adolescent Psychology*, vol. 33, 237–247.

Zahavi, D. (1997). "Horizontal Intentionality and Transcendental Intersubjectivity." *Tijdschrift Voor Filosofie*, vol. 59, no. 2, 304–321.

Zahavi, D. (2014). *Self and Other: Exploring Subjectivity, Empathy, and Shame*. Oxford: Oxford University Press.

8

SEXUAL NORMALITY AND INTERCORPOREALITY

Introduction

In this chapter I am going to apply the notion of normality and intersubjectivity as discussed in the previous chapter, to the case of gender identity. My goal is to reflect critically on normality in order to overcome a polarizing and disembodied dichotomy. For this purpose I will conclude the chapter with a short digression on the notion of intercorporeality as a means of overcoming the dichotomy.

The chapter will be divided into three sections: first, an overview of how the normal is defined. Here I summarize and link to my previous discussion of empathy, intersubjectivity, and normality. In the second section I will focus on what is considered abnormal in terms of gender identity according to the DSM-IV and V. In the third section I will discuss the political implications of normality and abnormality as they pertain to Gender Identity Disorder.

What is Normality?

In the previous chapter the notion of normality emerged from the analysis of the intersubjective community whose constitution passes through a two-layered affective process involving time and empathy. In fact, normality results from the agreement of different layers of a common intersubjective compound. What I think it is important to emphasize here is that since these two layers are incarnated in a living body, they cannot be conceived of without an actual body, be it a simple physical object or a social whole (like family, tribe, city, nation).

Against Habermas' (1994) claim that phenomenology is at its base solipsistic, Zahavi (2012) argues that the ultimate ground for phenomenology is, in fact, an embodied intersubjectivity which is demonstrated by the work of phenomenologists who developed Husserl's ideas in an intersubjective direction like Stein, Scheler, Merleau-Ponty, and Schütz. For example: against the theory that considers empathy an effort to see the Other through a detached, analogizing lens, Scheler shows how in order to gain an access to other people's minds we need to see the Other as a lived body in its *Ausdruckenheit* (expressivity; 1954, 261). In fact, as discussed in Chapter 3, the body is a psychophysical unity that tells something of itself to us.[1]

The intersubjective experience is what emerges from the discovery of my incarnated I that is given to me through movement. First, an individual can only be said to be "normal," in Husserl's sense, in the midst of and by virtue of a normal community within the life world.[2] My I emerges as distinct from my surrounding intersubjective matter when I discover that I am the subject/owner of one action but not another one. The way in which I realize about my own self originates in my awareness of my being intimately interwoven with others' bodies and my being responsible of my own physical acts. This bodily understanding of my own nature happens through time.[3]

As explained in the previous chapter, I gain access to what I am through the synthetic activity of time, and it is in time that I find the intersection of intentions (passive, active, and practical) in which time itself originates. It is time, meant as a synthetic concept, that generates what we physically are in space. In the next section I will discuss how crucial time is as a diagnostic whereby the DSM measures the sexual abnormal behavior in relation to gender.[4]

Whereas normality for Husserl indicates "concordance" (*Einstimmigkeit*) with regard to certain objects (Husserl, 1973, section 21) within a certain period of time, or, practical familiarity with expected experiences (Hua IV, section 59), abnormality stands for a lack of certain faculties and capacities to relate to the world in the expected or outlined time (Hua I, section 55).[5] In a text dated January, 1931 (Hua XXXXII), Husserl refers to normality and abnormality as the two levels that explain the incarnated phenomenon of the world (*Weltphänomens*).[6] As Steinbock (1994, 208) remarks:

> By normal and abnormal, Husserl does not mean medicinal or psychological normality; rather, he evokes a normality and

abnormality on a constitutional level, namely, the sense constitution of the lived body, objects, worlds, traditions, etc., as concordant, optimal, typical and familiar.

Our experience in the world is not normal per se, it is a concordance of sense that we assign within a given time through the experiences of our bodies. For us, normality and abnormality are liminal concepts framed within the horizon of primordial bodily experiences. We use the term normality to label the sense of an experience that is the result of an intentional modification of our primordial home; what remains outside of this range of experience is considered abnormal. The phenomenon of abnormality is part of the phenomenon of normality and vice-versa. Normality is an accepted concretion (*Typik*) or a sedimentation of meanings that are originally neither normal nor abnormal (Hua XXXXII, 48). They represent a "home-world," to use Steinbock's language, that is mutually and primordially constituted.

In that sense, normality is a synthetic social concept that while not originating in clinical psychology, is often incorporated by psychology as a kind of clinical label. "Every clinician"—wrote Verhaeghe (1994, 35)—has experienced in his life a certain amount of anxiety, depression, relationship problems, problems in growing up, etc. As long as what he encounters in his client is situated within the limits of his own experience, he will consider this more than likely as "normal." However, if what she encounters in her client is situated outside her quantitative field of experiences, she might diagnose it as pathological and if it is situated outside her qualitative field of experiences, the diagnosis will become "psychosis."

In the next sections I will provide an example for what is considered abnormal in clinical work in order to show how this notion can affect our identity in daily life.

Social Normality

"Social Ontology" (Hua XIII, 102) or "descriptive sociology" (Hua XIII, 102f.) is the name of the region of Being constituted by "social unities" (Hua IV, 196; VIII, 198; XIII, 99–104; XXVII, 22, 27) that are connected by a common "intentional sociology" (Hua XXXIX, 389), or an "intersubjective and collective intentionality" (cf., e.g., Hua XIV, 196ff. and Husserl 1923). According to Husserl all truth and all beings have their intentional source in this form of transcendental intersubjective sociality (cf. Husserl 1999: 156) which constitutes the material source of all the meanings one uses with respect to actions and decisions in one's daily life. Husserl states that normally the constitution of what one considers absolutely objective must be understood as the culmination of an ongoing intersubjective intentional process of cultivating newer systems of norms at ever higher levels (Husserl 1973: 421). As I wrote in Chapters 1, 2, and 3 there is an ascending process from the passive matter to the intentional meaning-giving activity that passes through the awakening of practical intentionality; this ascension is primordially situated within an intersubjective web of intentions because originally the passive matter is not owned by a specific individual, and it is through the awakening of each singular body that new systems of norms and meanings can be created.

For example, a variety of studies documented how women who experienced miscarriages or unexpected early deaths of their children felt inexplicably ashamed and responsible for their loss,[7] as if it was their personal inadequacy that prevented nature from fulfilling itself through them. From a phenomenological point of view this feeling seems to be justified by the intercorporeal sense of normality embedded in the passive intersubjective matter mentioned above. During pregnancy a woman's body seems to become a collective good. Pregnant women are invested with the powerful gift of nature that makes them a sort of fertility goddess. If this power elicits care and attention on the one hand, it deprives the person from her own intimate space on the other. For this reason if it happens that they "fail" to complete the pregnancy, their resilience is strongly weakened. They experience a block in recovering or constituting the meaning of the event because they did not own fully their bodies and the meanings they assigned to it are strictly interwoven with the instinctive selfishness of the species. The work they would need to do in order to overcome the sense of shame is to break this unsaid intercorporeal ownership, become aware of its norms, and dismiss that passive intercorporeal power received by the community in order to work on a process of meaning recovery; this would help them to constitute new meanings for themselves as individual embodied monads.

As Carr (1987) remarks,

> The human being lives in the norm insofar as she becomes aware of it as a norm. The normal style of life as the style of communal life is not only a fact for her, but an obligation of being.

Our sense of normality is embedded in the style of the communal life in which we are obligated to live our daily life; recovering the meaning of that sense of normality requires on the one hand an act of monadological reflection, but on the other it frees us from an implied sense of normality that can prevent us from constituting authentic meanings. Normality is a state of affairs that is built upon pre-predicative and predicative, passive and active, material and spiritual layers. According to Zahavi (1994) normality is a form of intersubjective agreement by means of which the totality of functioning subjects (96) agree on the meanings (predicative layer) given to the affections (pre-predicative layer) that stem from the awakenings of the I-thou (practical intention). Life can be seen as a habitual acquisition of a foreign normality (82) arising from the interplay between passive, active, and practical intentionality (Husserl, Ms. C 17–15).

In that sense, as Gyllenhammer remarked, the "Body is the realm of norm mediation or optimization" (2009, 53, 54) from which we derive the material for our political, social, and personal struggles about what should be defined as normal within a living standard of motivations (55). As Hart (2006) notes, within the intersubjective community I am responsible for my passivity (66, 67) and for the shape of meanings that my body would passively convey in my interaction with other bodies. I believe that each one of us has the responsibility to become aware of this passivity and to move—through the aid of fantasy and courage—toward the active meanings that best fit in the society in which one would dream to live. In fact, we need to use our imagination in order to reach domains that would seem impossible for us to reach; and we need courage in order to pursue an exploration which goes far beyond our comfort zone.

If we become aware of the natural functioning (*fungierend Leiblichkeit*) that will attract a number of incarnated meanings that will define our and other people's norms. If our core is strong then we will not be defined by meanings that we do not recognize as true, but we will accept as a defining force only what fits in our core. The meanings attached to these norms can be accepted and recognized as valid or not; yet it is through the active and aware exercise of this acceptance that we have a chance to be ourselves within the community. If we have the courage to expand in awareness the boundaries of our functioning before the intersubjective agreement shrinks us into a small space and makes us blind to its possible new horizons, we might find the meanings that suit us the best.

A Case of Social Normality and Abnormality

If we apply this analysis to the theme of gender identity we can see how even a layer as intimate as one's sexual identity can be restrained and shrunk within the limits of intersubjective societal norms.

While in the previous editions of DSM gender incongruence was considered an identity disorder and treated as such, in the new edition of the DSM (2013) a new committee gathered and decided to replace the word identity with incongruence and disorder with disphoria. (Hansell and Damour, 2008) Incongruence, they wrote,

> is a descriptive term that better reflects the core of the problem: an incongruence between, on the one hand, what identity one experiences and/or expresses and, on the other hand, how one is expected to live based on one's assigned gender (usually at birth).
> *(Meyer-Bahlburg, 2002; Winters, 2005)*

The word "dysphoria" was chosen in order to indicate the profound state of dismay and uneasiness following the acknowledgment of the incongruence.

Before this revision anyone who did not feel happy with his/her body might have been diagnosed with this kind of disorder. The following two cases provide interesting examples of what was classified as abnormal prior to 2013:

1. Phil is a 35-year-old male suffering from gender identity disorder. This condition exists when an individual displays symptoms of distress related to his or her physical gender. In his early years, the patient suggested that his male features would fall off and reveal his feminine body, and when he entered adolescence, he began having sexual encounters with other males. The patient indicates that he never felt comfortable with his sexual identity and became intimately involved with women that he either admired or envied (Hansell and Damour, 2008). Phil obviously suffers from a conflict between his physical gender and the gender he identifies as, and is very uncomfortable with his male body.

2. The patient is a highly educated and successful professor of anthropology. As a child he found himself more interested in playing with girls and dolls. He had a very close relationship with his mother and found it easier to make friends with girls than boys. His father was an abusive alcoholic who regularly abused Phil's mother. Phil expressed to his parents in early childhood that his male genitals would fall off, and he spent time with a child therapist because his parents were alarmed by his belief. In his early teen years, Phil expressed his attraction of other males to his mother. She was very supportive of the possibility that Phil was a homosexual. When he

came out as a homosexual, he experimented with same-sex relationships, but never felt fully comfortable with his own male body. He experimented with cross-dressing, and portraying a feminine role with his sexual partners, but continued to lack internal happiness with his gender.

An important commonality is that both cases refer to "A disruption in an individual's gender identity, which is directly related to his or her sexuality" (Hansell and Damour, 2008). A gender identity disorder is identified on the basis of two specific variables: sexual ease, meant as the harmony that one's individual feeling in relation to her biological body; and gender—that is the individual's psychological sense of congruence with being male or female (Hansell and Damour, 2008). According to the previous DSM definition of gender disorder, individuals *suffering from* gender identity disorder may act and present themselves as members of the opposite sex, and may display symptoms like *altered choice* of sexual partners, mannerisms, behavior, choice of attire, and self-concept (Hansell and Damour, 2008).

In this latter description of gender disorder, terms like "suffering" or "altered choice" stand out to me as moral assumptions that overshadow the attempt to arrive at a clinical description. I propose that if the person would be left free to discover her identity without being forced into a label, I do not think that any suffering would be involved. The suffering comes from the isolating path in which a person would be left to live in case she has the courage to stick to her choice to live an authentic life. Second, the "altered choice" is "altered" only in relation to an intersubjective standard that does not necessarily match with one's psychological identity.

Moreover, according to Hansell and Damour (2008, 1) the gender identity is a disorder if the "identity conflicts continue over time." The symptoms "can vary depending on the subject's age and social environment. Children suffering from gender identity disorder can display symptoms ranging from a disgust for his or her genitals."

Standing by this description, I believe that in this case it is very difficult to draw a neat line between the average adolescent and a diagnosable one, given the growing number of adolescents ashamed of the shape, smell, size, function, and so forth of their genitals. What are the criteria we can use to distinguish what is diagnosable from what is not?

Another symptom that the DSM lists is based on the sense of sadness that comes from "being rejected by peers." I find this symptom again very common to a large number of adolescents. Those who experience this feeling of sadness might grow with "a belief that he or she will grow up to become the opposite sex, and state that he or she wants to be the opposite sex" (Hansell and Damour, 2008).

To what point we state that social integration is normal and functional? I remember once I had in my class a student who seemed to be perfectly integrated in the social environment of the class. Yet, half-jokingly one day she told me that she wanted to have a "thigh gap" and she would have put herself on a very harsh diet in order to reach that shape. When I met her again after the summer break, I was just shocked to see how much weight she lost. Certainly, she was very happy with her new shape and she felt more integrated with her group of peers. Hence my question is which desire is diagnosable according to our intersubjective sense of normality and which one is not? Who are our peers? Is breast surgery augmentation to be considered abnormal? Is my student's behavior—which is very common for an adolescent—normal?

The article (Hansell and Damour, 2008) continues in citing the case in which "adults suffering from the gender disorder may dress like the opposite sex, feel alone and isolated." In this case I think that it is our social responsibility to avoid anyone feeling isolated and stigmatized if they choose to dress differently. These people, they continue, "suffer from anxiety or depression" which, from my point of view, is the most reasonable result that one can expect from a state of isolation and unreasonable stigmatization. Some people described in the article "show a desire to live as a member of the opposite sex, and show a desire to eliminate his or her genitals"; in this case, I recognize that the desire is more specific and maybe disrupting. It is still questionable why breast augmentation/reduction surgery, hymen reconstruction to restore virginity, or ribs removal to gain a thinner waist are considered less disruptive. What I want to state here is that the criterion we choose to draw a line between what is normal and abnormal are highly questionable.

To conclude in the commentary of the DSM's definition of the gender identity disorder they state that a two-year timeframe is sufficient to determine if the person can be diagnosed with the disorder. "This time [the journal continues] helps clinicians to determine if the individual is actually suffering from gender identity disorder, or another disorder that has similar desires" (Hansell and Damour, 2008).

I think it is important here to emphasize the crucial role that time plays in the meaning-giving activity that we operate within the intersubjective community. The minimum amount of time considered necessary to assign a meaning in the form of a reliable diagnosis (a clinical intersubjective norma) was two years in 2000, and in 2013 six months. It seems to me that our actual problem with time is not growing older, but losing meaning; if our awareness does not arise in a way that is sufficiently rapid to assign a convincing meaning to our own matter within the intersubjective realm, then someone else will do it on our behalf and we do not know if that meaning actually fits in our Being.

Yet, even if the definition of gender identity disorder is stated with clarity and supported with a number of seemingly objective symptoms, the article concludes by stating that "the causes of gender identity disorder are not known." This statement seems to me to imply a mechanistic view of human beings meant as machines to be fixed rather than integral wholes of meaning. In fact, I think that not understanding the cause of problematic lived-experience is not a negligible step to solve the problem; causes constitute the rational and understandable structure of the phenomenon. How can one consider abnormal a phenomenon as intimate as sexual identity if the phenomenon itself is not understandable? Could one take a neutral position instead? Is the label of normality and abnormality based on the level of disruption that it generates within an intersubjective system rather than the disruptiveness it might entail for the individual? If so, that would lead to an ethics in which the insurgence of any variation would be labeled as wrong and abnormal and only that which serves the survival of the intersubjective community would be finally accepted and integrated as normal.

In the two stories reported above, the implied meanings were useful for the growth of our intersubjective understanding. Trying to unfold and activate each meaning is all of our responsibilities.

Do We Need to be Abnormal?

Bartlett and colleagues (2000) reconsidered the meaning of gender identity disphoria and recommended the removal of the label "gender identity disorder" from the DSM by arguing that

> children who experience a sense of inappropriateness in the culturally prescribed gender role of their sex but do not experience discomfort with their biological sex should not be considered to have GID. Because of flaws in the DSM-IV definition of mental disorder, and limitations of the current research base, there is insufficient evidence to make any conclusive statement regarding children who experience discomfort with their biological sex.

(753)

Moreover, in 2007 Drescher (2013) was appointed by the American Psychiatric Association Board of Trustees to serve as a member of the DSM-5 Workgroup on Sexual and Gender Identity Disorders. One section of the article he wrote on this experience had the title "Stigma Versus Access to Care." The main point he defended here was about the necessity to keep this phenomenon in the DSM as a diagnosable disorder. Its removal, in fact, would have caused an increasing loss of care for those who needed psychological and physical assistance in adjusting to their gender.[8]

Hence, even if the scientific community unfolded the meaning of this phenomenon that makes it intersubjectively acceptable for the society, this "dysphoria" has still to hold the vestigia of a mild abnormality because if it were normal the sanitary infrastructure would not care about it, i.e., actual care (counseling, etc.) of whatever quality would not be provided for young people who are suffering. For this reason, even if Drescher found the decision to remove gender identity disorder from the DSM fully agreeable, he realized that if he had accepted the change, he would have penalized all those people who need access to care. Therefore he listed a number of reasons in support of such a decision and mentioned the changes that I cited at the beginning of this section in order to redefine this phenomenon (i.e., "disphoria" instead of "disorder" and "incongruence" instead of "identity"):

> Arguments for retention of the diagnosis include: (1) the need for children with Gender Dysphoria to have access to care, which is often complex and involves treatment of both the family and social environment; (2) increased efforts to narrow clinical criteria to exclude gender atypical behavior unrelated to a diagnosis of Gender Dysphoria; and (3) the need to make it clear to clinicians that the gender diagnoses of childhood do not progress directly into the gender diagnoses of adolescence and adulthood. In fact, most children who meet criteria for a gender diagnosis grow up to be gay rather than transgender.
>
> *(2013, 9)*

Drescher's decision as representative of the meaning that DSM-V workgroup on Sexual and Gender Identity Disorders decided to assign to this disorder is quite clear. Intersubjective society can protect people only if they are abnormal and subject to stigmatization; it can offer protection by isolation, stigmatization, and social care.[9] One needs to be abnormal in order to be taken care of. Even if gender dysphoria is not recognized anymore as a disorder, society needs to maintain that category in place even though its sense does not match fully the felt sense that those who experience that "dysphoria" would assign.

Unfortunately, in accepting such category, even if empty, one is obliged to accept also a specific package of meanings that will affect their life. At that point the person will feel at best marginalized and somewhat detached from the intersubjective web to which she belongs, at worse her sense of intimacy in relation to the web of meanings would be disrupted by the pre-given package of meanings that are assigned to her (see Chapters 3 and 5 on this point).

This social solution seems to encourage a schizoid society in which people are only given the choice between living a disembodied or a miserable life. The forced sacrifice of meaning for care is unjust in that it cannot lead to a well-balanced social life. It seems that one needs to be abnormal and stigmatized in order to get closer to herself; but the intimacy that is reached is not fully true because it is continuously undermined by the disruption of meanings that administrative paperwork and routine interviews might bring in.[10]

This behavior results in a society of disembodied isolated victims in which at best the abnormal-victims are looked at by the normal-jailors with moralistic compassion, or at worse with moralistic superiority.[11] Liberal arts, social workers, psychologists, have the responsibility of mediating this meaning within the society in a way that might feel more truthful and authentic.

The Norms of Love

These two last sections showed how agapic love might manifest itself through norms that can in fact harm the harmonious well-being of the individuals instead of enhancing it. On this point, Drummond wrote "it is unclear (...) how an absolute ought and an absolute love can be correlates (...) we cannot be commanded to love, but only to respect someone as Kant reminds us" (Drummond, 2015, 66). Agapic love is not the same as intimate or erotic love (which we discussed in the previous chapters). Agapic love is a form of respect that cannot be translated into any specific ought. "So respect, rather than an absolute love, would be the appropriate affective response to an absolute ought (such as the moral law)" (Drummond, 2015, 66).

For Husserl agapic love represents an absolute ought when it is capable of conveying the essential lawfulness (and not normativity) that underlies and constitutes society. There is an important difference between norms and laws; as Husserl shows in the Prolegomena, norms depend on and are founded in laws, but laws are independent of these norms. Laws express an essential necessity that norms translate in prescriptive form. Intersubjective pre-predicative validation acknowledges a lawfulness or a group of belongingness that is, afterwards, expressed predicatively through norms and intersubjective normality. Love is an absolute lawful call to the material substrate, but the norm through which we answer that call is nourished by respect and responsibility. I argue therefore that the ought (love) is not a command, but an absolute necessity. This necessity is not prescriptive because I can have the freedom to accept or reject this ought—in other words, to decide whether and how to love or not to love my neighbor.

In the case of gender identity disphoria, agapic love would command respect toward those who seek ongruence between their bodies and their assigned sexuality. This respect can eventually be translated in a number of norms that tentatively define the lawfulness that describe the phenomenon. "Amor ipse notitia est" Gregory the Great wrote—"Love is itself knowledge." Love shows the essence of things in a practical way as they present themselves to us and according to their mutual relationship. It is up to us to make an effort to adjust ourselves to the meanings that these fluid relationships show.

According to Drummond, social roles do not express love in itself; rather, they express individual responsibility for myself and others (Drummond, 2015, 67; but also Drummond, 2010). It is not the absolute love embodied in a vocational commitment that identifies the ought, the obligation, but the recognition of respect, to which all agents are entitled by virtue of their capacities for thinking, feeling, and acting. This recognition underlies our social relationships and is required for us to secure those material goods for all within a well-regulated community so that first order goods may be virtuously pursued.

I agree with Drummond (2015) on this point. If love becomes a social obligation our choice and genuinely ethical responsibility to own our matter would be erased and our authentic consent would be divorced from our behavior. While Hart insists that social harmony as a teleological determinism is implied by Husserl's theory (1959), I think that the freedom of reflection and interpretation remains, and this makes the direction of the matter less deterministic. The reflective quality of love is exactly what makes the choice the essential core of free love.

Since love is a social bond, we might run the risk of creating a totalitarian society in which every personal feature is erased in virtue of an essential command that leaves no choice and therefore no space for personal responsibility.

If we collapse the essence of a lived-experience, in this case love, to an exclusively normative level, we might fall into the illusion of feeling that whatever we command others to do is true—even if we command love through genocide (which is what has happened more than once in human history by claiming love for one's nation, race, social status, etc.). What is essential, is the ought that love represents can be normatively translated into responsibility, vocational response, respect and many other actions that can be normatively expressed; yet, its essence will always remain an unknown core that calls for more precise predicates and a more defining foundational relationship. The essential level can never be exhausted by the normative and practical one; at that essential level, love is an absolute.

Intercorporeality, a Suggestion

Here I will list four reasons why I think that the notion of normality might benefit by being linked to the idea of intercorporeality.

First, if we go straight to the core of what normality is—that is, an intersubjective and intercorporeal agreement between pre-predicative and predicative layers—we would gain a better sense of ourselves in the community in a less moralistic fashion. Adopting the point of view of intercorporeality would make us more responsible and aware of what we bring in the "orchestra of our life." If "my body," as Merleau-Ponty writes, "becomes a means of understanding them (others), my corporality becomes a comprehending power of their corporality—I regain the final meaning (*Zwecksinn*) of other's people behavior, because my body is capable of achieving the same goals" (1962, 42). In being aware of the use of my body I use and understand Others' body, all that I do with my body becomes a means to understand and to constitute oneself and the Others. In this way I will always be responsible for what is normal as much as the Other is. It is as if the Other and I were playing together the same symphony; each of us follows a different section of the score, but each one of us directly affects the Other and is directly affected by others, and the sense of each part is completed by the others. For example, seeing someone rant and rave on the street elicits a number of feelings whose range goes from compassion to a sense of moral judgment and superiority. If we were able to set aside these feelings and focus on the important question—What did I do that brought this man to sleep on the street? How can my daily life better impact the life of this person?—we might contribute to the betterment of the society. As Merleau-Ponty wrote "The normal and the pathological can be considerably enriched by the contact of one with the other" (Merleau-Ponty, 1968, 64).

Second, meanings can actually change organic matter as much as organic matter can change meanings. If we keep a position of wonder and never-ending meaning-giving activity in relation to our incarnated world, we would allow for a richer range of meanings to shape ours and other's people being in life. On the other hand, if we accept rigid definitions of disembodied meaning, we might fall into a schizoid life in which we actually lose our bodies.

Third, being aware of the embodied interconnection between human beings would lead to a diagnosis, (which from Greek means "knowing through" an intersubjective web), that does not stigmatize and isolate, but calls for the best outcome. Accepting a label of normality that is completely enslaved to a Zeitgeist and can in any moment isolate people from each other would lead to a life of desperation and anxiety. Using responsibly our freedom to explore ourselves and the meanings that we assign to our life is a good way to find a real diagnosis; that is, a real understanding of what is in our best interest.

The fourth and last point, according to a phenomenological point of view reasoning in terms of intercorporeality would foster the never-ending and foundationless search that characterizes the phenomenological attitude. The label of abnormality/normality would end any possible quest and increase the anxiety and sense of desperation in which the person receiving the label would live, because it means that the meanings defining her life are wrong. If we acknowledge the interconnection and its never-ending unfolding of meanings the people marked with any label might be feel freer to take a step forward in the direction of a deeper sense of happiness and stability. As Buber (1963) writes: "I, as the ego, have constituted and am continually constituting as a phenomenon" (section 45, 99/130).

I run into my immanent temporality and, with it, my existence in the form of an open infiniteness, that of a stream of subjective processes. (section 46, 102/132) ... I exist with an essentially necessary all-inclusiveness and without which I could not exist. They include (among others) the mode of existence in the form of a certain all-embracing life of some sort or other, that of existence in the form of the continuous self-constitution of that life's own processes, as temporal within an all-embracing time, and so forth" (section 46, 103/132).

To conclude, even if the political discourse seems to need the dichotomy normal and abnormal, as shown in the case of gender identity theory, I think that it might be helpful to start thinking through the primordial origin of these categories in order to exploit its real meanings and free human beings from the burden of abnormality and social control.

Conclusion

In this chapter I analyzed the meaning of normality and abnormality in relation to the notion of intercorporeality. I applied what emerged from my previous analysis to the case of gender identity disorder in order to show how a disembodied meaning of intersubjectivity leads to a definition of normality that obliges the individual to choose between identity or care. For this reason, as a concluding note in the chapter, I proposed to use the notion of intercorporeality as complementary to construing an embodied idea of normality.

Notes

1 As stated by Merleau-Ponty we find the Other when we find ourselves in the world. Or for Levinas the Other is manifest to us in his elusiveness and inaccessibility (1987, 94). For Scheler, we can be able to empathetically experience other minds (1954, 9, 220).

2 See "Zur Phaenomenologie der Intersubjektivitaet" (Husserliana, vol. 14), Beilage 1 from 1921; and "Zur Phaenomenologie der Intersubjektivitaet" (Husserliana, vol. 15), 619, 83; "Zur Phaenomenologie der Intersubjektivitaet" (Husserliana, vol. 15), 142, 15.

3 As Merleau-Ponty remarks:

> To analyse time is not to follow out the consequences of a pre-established conception of subjectivity, it is to gain access, through time, to its concrete structure. If we succeed in understanding the subject, it will not be in its pure form, but by seeking it at the intersection of its dimensions. We need, therefore, to consider time itself, and it is by following through its internal dialectic that we shall be led to revise our idea of the subject.
>
> *(PhP, 410–411/469–470)*

4 As the article shows:

> The 6 month duration was introduced to make at least a minimal distinction between very transient and persistent GI. The duration criterion was decided upon by clinical consensus. However, there is no clear empirical literature supporting this particular period (e.g., three months vs. six

months or six months vs. 12 months). There was, however, consensus among the group that a lower-bound duration of six months would be unlikely to yield false positives. The minimum amount of time requested for a reliable diagnosis was in 2000 two years, in 2013 six months.

5 For example, Foucault wrote:

> The history of psychiatry in the 19th and 20th centuries is history of the continuous attempt and failure to isolate functional area of the psyche which would give a conceptual unity and clarity to the differential clinic of psychopathological disorders.
>
> *(F., The Birth of the Clinic, 1973, passim)*

Besides Foucault, Szasz compared psychiatry with witchcraft and slavery; and devoted a book (if not an entire career) on the definition of the myth of mental illness. Although R. J. Laing rejected the label of anti-psychiatric movement, like Szasz he took a position that was very close to the professionals belonging to that group. He expanded and investigated the meaning of what normality means beyond the definition provided by psychiatry. Moreover in a less revolutionary way, Guggenbühl-Craig (2015) in his "Eros on Crutches" commented on the dichotomizing way in which clinical psychology organizes psychopathy and morality in its way to define what is normal. Fromm even coined the expression pathology of normalcy to define the bias in which the practicioner can easily fall: The "pathology of normalcy" rarely

> deteriorates to graver forms of mental illness because society produces the antidote against such deterioration. When pathological processes become socially patterned, they lose their individual character. On the contrary, the sick individual finds himself at home with all other similarly sick individuals. The whole culture is geared to this kind of pathology and arranges the means to give satisfactions which fit the pathology. The result is that the average individual does not experience the separateness and isolation the fully schizophrenic person feels. He feels at ease among those who suffer from the same deformation; in fact, it is the fully sane person who feels isolated in the insane society-and he may suffer so much from the incapacity to communicate that it is he who may become psychotic
>
> *(The Anatomy of Human Destructiveness, 1973, 356.*
> *New York: Holt, Rinehart, and Winston)*

6 Hua XXXXII, 224: "Normalität und Anomalität konstituiert Erweiterung der Endlichkeit. Die sozialen Gliederungen, Schichtungen. Das Sich-Verstehen in der Stufe, das Sich-Nichtverstehen von Personen verschiedener Stufe. Ausbildung der verstehenden Einfühlung."

7 See, for example, Parsons, K. (2010). "Feminist Reflections on Miscarriage, in Light of Abortion." *International Journal of Feminist Approaches to Bioethics*, vol. 3, no. 1, 1–22.

8 The conclusion of his work was:

> Retention of the gender diagnoses (to maintain access to care), both in children and in adolescents and adults; Name change from Gender Identity Disorder to Gender Dysphoria (to reduce stigma); Separate chapter for Gender Dysphoria which is no longer bundled with the Paraphilias and Sexual Dysfunction (to reduce stigma); The addition of a post-transition specifier to be used in the context of continuing treatment procedures that serve to support the new gender assignment (a kind of "exit clause" from the diagnosis, which reduces stigma, when the post-transition individual is no longer gender dysphoric but still requires access to care for ongoing hormone treatment); and Narrower diagnostic criteria to reduce false positives (to reduce stigma).

9 Foucault, of course, already put his finger on this point in his *History of Sexuality* (1984) and *History of Madness* (1961/2006).
10 In her PhD dissertation a student of mine, Kelly Wordshworth, usefully described this dynamic as it is practiced also for veterans affected by PTSD.
11 The Frankfurt school (Marcuse, for example, in his *Eros and Civilization*) had shed light on the social need for labels as a means to bring to existence a reality that otherwise would not even exist. The problem here is that that label which defines the identity of a person, helps the person to access to care only at the price of preventing her to find a genuine meaning to assign to her life.

Bibliography

Bartlett, N. H., Vasey, P.L., and Bukowski, W. M. (2000). "Is Gender Identity Disorder in Children a Mental Disorder?" *Sex Roles*, vol. 43, 753–785.
Buber, M. (1963). *Pointing the Way*. New York: Harper Torchbooks.
Carr, D. (1987). *Interpreting Husserl. Critical and Comparative Studies*. Dordrecht/ Boston/London: Kluwer Academic Publishers.
Drescher, J. (2013). "Controversies in Gender Diagnosis." *LGBT Health*, vol. 1, no. 1, 9–13.
Drummond, J. (2010). "Self-responsibility and Eudaimonia," in Philosophy, Phenomenology, Sciences: Essays in Commemoration of Edmund Husserl, 411–430, (eds. Ierna, C., Jacobs, H., and Mattens, F.). Dordrecht: Springer.
Drummond, J. (2015). "Exceptional Love," *Phenomenologica*, vol. 216, 51–69.
Foucault, M. (1961/2006). *History of Madness*, (ed. Khalfa, J. and trans. Murphy, J.). New York: Routledge.
Foucault, M. (1984). *History of Sexuality, vol. 1,* (trans. Hurley, R.). New York: Random House.
Glynos, J. and Stavrakakis, Y. (2002). *Lacan and Science*. London: Routledge.
Guggenbühl-Craig, A. (2015). *Marriage Is Dead, Long Live Marriage!* (trans. Stein, M.). Kindle edition: Springer Publications.

Gyllenhammer, P. (2009). "Normality in Husserl and Foucault." *Research in Phenomenlogy*, vol. 39, 52–68.

Habermas, J. (1994). *Postmetaphysical Thinking*. Cambridge, MA: The MIT Press

Hansell, J. and Damour, L. (2008). *Abnormal Psychology* (2nd edn.). Hoboken, NJ: Wiley.

Hart, J. (1959). 'We, Representation and War-resistance: Some Para-Husserlian Reflections." *Zeitschrift für philosophische Forschung*, vol. 13, 127–141.

Hart, J. (2006). "The Absolute Ought and the Unique Individual," *Husserl Studies*, vol. 22, no. 1, 223–240.

Husserl, E. (1973). *Zur Phänomenologie der Intersubjektivität I, Husserliana XIII*. The Hague: Martinus Nijhoff.

Husserl, E. (2014). *Grenzprobleme der Phänomenologie. Analysen des Unbewusstseins und der Instinkte. Metaphysik. Späte Ethik (Texte aus dem Nachlass 1908–1937)*, (ed. Sowa, R. and Vongehr, T.). New York, Springer.

Levinas, E. (1987). *Time and the Other*. Pittsburgh: Duquesne University Press.

Marcuse, H. (1966). *Eros and Civilization*. Boston: Beacon Press.

Merleau-Ponty, M. (1962). *Phenomenology of Perception*, (trans. Smith, C.). London and New York: Routledge.

Merleau-Ponty, M. (1968/1964). *The Visible and the Invisible*, (trans. Lingis, A.). Evanston: Northwestern University Press.

Meyer-Bahlburg, H. F. L. (2002). "Gender Identity Disorder in Young Boys: A Parent- and Peer-based Treatment Protocol." *Clinical Child Psychology and Psychiatry*, vol. 7, 360–376.

Parsons, K. (2010). "Feminist Reflections on Miscarriage, in Light of Abortion." *International Journal of Feminist Approaches to Bioethics*, vol. 3, no. 1, 1–22.

Scheler, M. (1954). *The Nature of Sympathy*. London: Routledge & Kegan Paul.

Steinbock, A. J. (1994). "Homelessness and the Homeless Movement: A Clue to the Problem of Intersubjectivity." *Human Studies*, vol. 17, no. 2, 203–223.

Verhaeghe, P. (1994). *Klinische Psykodiagnostik vanuit Lacans Diskoursetheorie*. Gent: Idesca.

Winters, K. (2005). "Gender Dissonance: Diagnostic Reform of Gender Identity Disorder for Adults." *Journal of Psychology & Human Sexuality*. vol. 17, no. 34, 71–89.

Zahavi, D. (1994). "Husserl's Phenomenology of the Body." *Études Phénoménologiques*, vol. 10, no. 19, 63–84.

Zahavi, D. (1997). "Horizontal Intentionality and Transcendental Intersubjectivity." *Tijdschrift Voor Filosofie*, vol. 59, no. 2, 304–321.

Zahavi, D., Luft, S. and Overgaard, O. (2012). *The Routledge Companion to Phenomenology*. London: Routledge.

INDEX

Krueger, J.W. 42

Laing, R.J. 153n5
Lasch, C. 82
Lee, N. 10, 36, 61
living body 46, 47, 59
Logical Investigations (Husserl) 12, 13, 14–15, 62, 91
longitudinal intentionality 116–17, 119–20
lower and higher spirit 6, 54–8
Luo, T.Y. 77–8

McDowell, J. 70
marital rape 77, 83n4, 84n5
masochism, sexual 5, 41–51
Melle, U. 126, 134n20
Merleau-Ponty, M. 46, 51n4, 113, 131n3, 139, 150, 151, 152n3
mind-body unit 46–7, 51n4
miscarriage 141
moods 96
Moore, T. 51n3, 81
moral freedom 80–2
Moran, D. 55
motility 46
motivational foundations of love 129
motivations 28, 55–6, 97, 98–9, 100

Nagel, T. 43
nature 33, 45, 51n4, 55, 92, 113
Neu, J. 89, 94
noema 16, 22n15
non-spontaneous synthesis 33, 47–8, 49
normality 8, 121–5, 138–52, 153n5; community of love 125–7; gender identity 139, 142–8, 149, 152, 152n4, 154n8; intercorporeality and 150–2; Ipseity of agapic love 127–9; norms of love 148–50
not-operating willing 28–31

objectifying acts 14–15, 30, 95
objectivation 4–5, 14, 18–20
oblique empathy 120–1
obsessive-compulsive personality disorder 90
operating willing 28–31
organic body 47, 94
Othello's Syndrome 89–90, 101–2, 105
ought of love 127

paraphilia 5, 41–51

passive intentionality 33–4, 47–8, 57–8, 71–2, 91–7
passivity 17–20, 106n5
pathological jealousy 89–90, 101–2, 105
pathology of normalcy 153n5
personality disorders, jealousy and 89–90
perversion 5, 41–51
Phenomenology of the Social World (Schütz) 116
philia 3, 6, 54–66; instincts, habits, and values 61–6; lower and higher spirit 6, 54–8; wakefulness and consent 58–61; *see also* intimacy; jealousy
plastic sexuality 80–2
Plato 45
poetry 73–4
practical intentionality 4–5, 10–20, 34, 35, 45–50, 57–8, 71–2, 91–4, 113
pregnancy 104, 114, 141
pre-predicative and predicative intersubjectivity 7–8, 110–30, 138–52; affection of empathy 8, 112, 118–21, 123–4; affection of time 8, 112, 116–18, 121; community of love 125–7; gender identity 139, 142–8, 149, 152, 152n4, 154n8; intercorporeality 8, 112–15, 131n5, 141, 150–2; Ipseity of agapic love 127–9; normality and 123–5; norms of love 148–50
presuppositional foundations of love 129

rape 77–8, 79–80, 81, 83n4, 84n5
reciprocal supplementation 128
recursive structure of sexual existence 69–73
refusal 48
retention 116–17
Ruch, L.O. 77–8

sadism, sexual 5, 41–51
Sartre, J.-P. 43–5, 62, 70, 72–3, 80
Scheler, M. 139
schizophrenic spectrum 90, 108n12
Schuhmann, K. 126
Schütz, A. 116, 139
Sennett, R. 82
sexual assault 77–8, 79–80, 81, 83n4, 84n5
sexual life 5, 6–7, 27–37; existential sexuality 69–73; forced intimacy 7, 75–80, 83n4; gender identity 139, 142–8, 149, 152, 152n4, 154n8; intercorporeality and 113–14; moral

For Product Safety Concerns and Information please contact our EU
representative GPSR@taylorandfrancis.com
Taylor & Francis Verlag GmbH, Kaufingerstraße 24, 80331 München, Germany

www.ingramcontent.com/pod-product-compliance
Lightning Source LLC
Chambersburg PA
CBHW050519280326
41932CB00014B/2381